In Deadly Embrace

Letter from the General Editor

The Library of Arabic Literature makes available Arabic editions and English translations of significant works of Arabic literature, with an emphasis on the seventh to nineteenth centuries. The Library of Arabic Literature thus includes texts from the pre-Islamic era to the cusp of the modern period, and encompasses a wide range of genres, including poetry, poetics, fiction, religion, philosophy, law, science, travel writing, history, and historiography.

Books in the series are edited and translated by internationally recognized scholars. They are published in parallel-text and English-only editions in both print and electronic formats. PDFs of Arabic editions are available for free download. The Library of Arabic Literature also publishes distinct scholarly editions with critical apparatus.

The Library encourages scholars to produce authoritative Arabic editions, accompanied by modern, lucid English translations, with the ultimate goal of introducing Arabic's rich literary heritage to a general audience of readers as well as to scholars and students.

The publications of the Library of Arabic Literature are generously supported by Tamkeen under the NYU Abu Dhabi Research Institute Award G1003 and are published by NYU Press.

Philip F. Kennedy
General Editor, Library of Arabic Literature

About this Paperback

This paperback edition differs in a few respects from its dual-language hardcover predecessor. Because of the compact trim size the pagination has changed. Material that referred to the Arabic edition has been updated to reflect the English-only format, and other material has been corrected and updated where appropriate. For information about the Arabic edition on which this English translation is based and about how the LAL Arabic text was established, readers are referred to the hardcover.

In Deadly Embrace

Arabic Hunting Poems

BY

IBN AL-MUʿTAZZ

TRANSLATED BY

JAMES E. MONTGOMERY

FOREWORD BY

A. E. STALLINGS

VOLUME EDITOR

RICHARD SIEBURTH

NEW YORK UNIVERSITY PRESS
New York

NEW YORK UNIVERSITY PRESS
New York

Please contact the Library of Congress for Cataloging-in-Publication data.

ISBN: 9781479835997 (paperback)
ISBN: 9781479836024 (library ebook)
ISBN: 9781479836000 (consumer ebook)

New York University Press books are printed on acid-free paper, and their binding materials are chosen for strength and durability.

Series design and composition by Nicole Hayward.
Typeset in Adobe Text

Manufactured in the United States of America
10 9 8 7 6 5 4 3 2 1

For Natasha and Mark—and Rufus, too.

Like as the fearfull Foule
    within the Fawcons foote
Doth yeelde himselfe to die,
    and sees none other boote;
Even so dread I (my deare)
    least ruth in thee will want,
To me that am thy thrall,
    who, fearing death, doe pant . . .
The hart within my breast
    with trembling feare doth quake;
And save your love (my deare)
    nought can my torment slake.

GEORGE TURBERVILLE, *EPITAPHES, EPIGRAMS, SONGS AND SONETS* (1567)

A man is not feminized because he is inverted but because he is in love.

ROLAND BARTHES, *A LOVER'S DISCOURSE*

Contents

Acknowledgments

The Library of Arabic Literature (LAL) continues to inspire me with its vision, energy, commitment to quality and standards, and conviction that classical Arabic literary creativity has a rightful place in our chaotic world. I am grateful to all my friends and mentors on the project for their generosity, erudition, friendship, and support. I owe Phil Kennedy and Shawkat Toorawa, as well as the editorial board past and present, an immeasurable debt, personal as well as intellectual.

It is always a thrill to open a new shipment of LAL books and admire the professionalism, care, and attention to detail that go into every volume. Chip Rossetti, Lucie Taylor, Stuart Brown, Keith Miller, and Wiam El-Tamami are an amazing team of professionals with whom it is an honor to work and learn from.

Once again, it has been my distinct privilege and joy to have Richard Sieburth as my volume editor—his lightness of touch is evident in every translation in the book. I alone am responsible for the imponderables and infelicities.

I have worked on this book during the last six months as I recovered from a serious illness. Yvonne, Natasha, Sam, and Josh willed me on every step of the way. And Reggie, our Jack Russell, reminded me of the skill and patience needed to train nonhumans: his madcap sprints in pursuit of squirrels are a highlight of the fall season.

Foreword

A. E. STALLINGS

No doubt for as long as humans have hunted—in other words, for as long as there have been humans—the chase has been entwined in the imagination with desire and storytelling, and thus with poetry, mankind's original mode of utterance. We must assume that alongside prehistoric cave paintings and petroglyphs of hunted mammals, song were also sung, telling the tales of pre-dawn pursuit, the wielding of weapons, episodes of danger, and celebrations of triumph, beside a campfire fragrant with the aroma of smoking meat. As pastoralism and agriculture replaced this method of food gathering for most people, aristocrats of nearly all societies reserved for themselves aspects of this more ancient ritual, with its costly accoutrements of horses, hawks, hounds, and open spaces. In the modern era, the poetry of pursuit has largely gone to ground, in the covert metaphors of words like "haggard," or the dogged traces of similes.

Western literature perhaps does not have a specific lyric genre dealing with the chase, as Arabic poetry has, but readers like me coming at the thrilling poems of *In Deadly Embrace* from this different tradition will still recognize much of the terrain. The hunt features in many a simile in the *Iliad*, applied to kingly warriors, where men and dogs face lions or wild boars, though even in the Bronze Age lions were not a regular fixture of the Anatolian landscape. (Have the Homeric poems retained some sort of Near East memory of royal lion hunts as depicted in, say, the reliefs at Nineveh?) The

Odyssey has its hunting similes too, including, notably, the netting and trapping of migratory song birds, and the description of the boar hunt on Mount Parnassus in Odysseus's youth, complete with its pre-dawn setting out, the chorus of hounds, and the description of a sumptuous feast, albeit one that happens before rather than after the hunt. In the *Aeneid*, Dido and Aeneas consummate their doomed relationship on a hunt, when a rainstorm drives them into a cave. The hunt is a commonplace of the narratives of medieval Romances and the lyrics of troubadours. Perhaps the English poem most central to the entanglement of hunting and desire is Shakespeare's *Venus and Adonis*, widely popular in its time, with its amorous palfrey, its metaphors from falconry, its hounds and perilous boar hunt, and the goddess of Love herself lovelorn for a beautiful young hunter. In famous sonnets too, the pursuit of the beloved and the "thrill of the chase" are indivisible: "Whoso list to hunt, I know where is an hind."

But for Shakespeare, or Virgil for that matter, the hunt was largely a literary gesture, a trope. Perhaps that is why, reading these poems by a poet prince for whom hunting was one of life's occupations, I am taken not only by their elegance and sophistication, but by the freshness of eye witness, of precise observation, especially of a natural world now threatened, by dark desert nights undiminished by light pollution or artificial satellites, by herds of oryxes and gazelles and flocks of waterfowl. Ibn al-Muʿtazz probably could not envision a time where his quarry, the onager, the elegant Syrian wild ass, had gone extinct in the wild.

It is in startling and precise similes and metaphors that Ibn al-Muʿtazz conveys his world. Some of these similes are perhaps already polished tropes in Arabic, but one of the joys of reading poetry in translation is that the idioms of one language are fresh-minted coinages in another. A horse's hooves are like "goblets overturned," dogs are "meteor-bright" and dash like shooting stars. Those goblets delighted me with their rightness as a shape, but also their inversion—upside down they perhaps suggest the outpouring of intoxicating power. The stoop (precipitous dive) of a bird of prey is likened to a bucket falling down an old well, an image violent in its plummet and force, but also its shocking contrast of the sublime and meteoric with the quotidian, height with depth, air with water. A horse is faster than "water spilling from a jug" or "thoughts flashing in a mind." Montgomery, in his splendid translations, is both sumptuous and uncompromising in offering us the correct vocabulary for the hunt, especially the argot of falconry: not only "stoop" but "mantle," not only "goshawk" but "tiercel," and best of all "yarak," a word that entered English from Ottoman Turkish and which means, of a bird of prey, to be kept hungry and keen, ready to fly and in fine fettle. ("Even as an empty eagle, sharp by fast," as Shakespeare would put it.) Luckily there is also a useful glossary here. Fans of Helen Macdonald's *H is for Hawk* will be very much in their element.

While some of Ibn al-Muʿtazz's surprising similes may be traditional, others have the force of originality, even modernity. Consider a hoof that is black as a "foot/swollen with venom." Or take this description of dawn on the horizon, with an image that would not be out of place in Sylvia Plath's "Ariel":

> The western horizon turned as red
> as the lid of an inflamed eye.
> The horses reached water in the dark

(The fragment functions as a complete imagistic poem.) In other modern touches, the hooves of horses pit "the face/ of the earth with smallpox scars," the wind has "soft hands," and the talons of a hawk are like "thin, arched eyebrows." Elsewhere we have the visual wit—not to mention the translator's satisfying English cadence--of a gos "poised on the red glove,/ her wings raised like the sleeves of a busy man."

It is in the similes too that a rich, multicultural world is fleshed out for us, if one in which we might be made uncomfortable by casual mentions of slavery or the subordination of women. (Upon the poet's waking at the break of dawn, dreams "are divorced like wives.") Where English lacks vocabulary, Montgomery supplies us with the Arabic:

> I left before dawn, just as day broke,
> still wrapped in the jilbab
> night had buttoned over us, black as pitch
> like the skin of a naked Nubian.

A goshawk's lids are compared to "the fringes of a Christian's belt," Dawn "removes her niqab," a trained cheetah

> sits in her pillion, like a Turkish beauty
> captured by Arabs, kohl from her eyes
> smeared on her cheeks, dressed
> in a dazzling gown of jade and gold.

Classical Arabic poetry is invariably rhymed, often monorhymed. (The Western use of rhyme arguably stems from Arabic influence.) Largely, Montgomery eschews rhyming in these nimble translations, letting the images speak for themselves, but occasionally we get a flash of what the effect might be: "A bitch, meteor-bright./ Look—out of the blocks,/ her tread so light/ you'd think she was a star /exploding in the night." Wisely, I think, Montgomery avoids going all out on monorhymes, which, in English, with its economy of rhyme scarcity, would tend toward the sing-song and claustrophobic.

The swoops, dashes, and dots, the slashes and swerves, of Arabic calligraphy are essential to many of the poems' descriptions. Writing itself is perhaps the poet's central metaphor. The handsome variegated feathers of a bird of prey, with their bars and inky ticking, resemble a snake's patterned scales, a coat of mail, are dappled "as with bubbles of wine," but also often enough likened to the written word: "decorated with patterned letters" or "like a bright page flecked with tiny script." A hunting dog (?) seen from afar becomes a mere dash, a "black *maddah*/ drawn by a stylus," a "saker in yarak" is

> a brilliant hunter with her curved talons
> like a calligrapher's *nūns,* her mail
> brightly clad in a patterned cloak
> like loops of *lāms* on parchment
> or kohl penciled on eyelids.

(The kohl-penciled eyelids are another vertex where longing and poetry, hunting and desire, meet. One might picture such eyelids on the callipygian boys who serve as wine bearers at the post-hunting feast, themselves compared to the aching beauty of hawks.)

Hunting in the modern world is often, as it was in Ibn al-Muʿtazz's time, the prerogative of the rich. ("Tis no sport for peasants," as Byron would remind us.) Riding to hounds implies kennels and stables; and grouse shooting in the UK, for instance, is associated with huge, biodiversity-depleted estates, imported nonnative game birds, and avian destruction on an industrial scale. The experience, one imagines, of an Arab aristocratic in preindustrial times would have been much more in harmony with nature (though, no doubt, such hunting also exerted its pressures on wild ecosystems, as Nineveh's lion hunts had done, or Rome's exotic *venationes* in the Colosseum.) In the southern U.S. where I grew up, hunting—by which I mean the shooting of doves, or quail, or ducks, or wild turkey, or boar, or deer—is more a pursuit of regular folk. Many a weekend, my father, a professor-cum-outdoorsman, would get up before first light to go off into the woods or fields with his fishing or hunting buddies and come home with a mess of birds full of lead shot for my mother to pluck and prepare, or occasionally, if lucky, a winter's worth of venison for the freezer. His life would have had almost nothing in common with Ibn al-Muʿtazz, but he would have recognized in these poems the romance of the pre-dawn departure, the wagging dogs, the high-hearted comradery of men, the hunt-furnished feast, and also the sacred bond between hunter and quarry. (This respect, however inadequate and transactional, is one not afforded to the animals that provide meat for us through battery hens and factory farms.) I always understood that meat came from animals, and that these animals were beautiful, and their blood was a sacrifice. One of my first memories, and one of the earliest stories told about me by my family, is of my sitting next to and stroking and mourning a beautiful brace of limp, iridescent-feathered mallards my father had brought home. Perhaps even then I was searching for similes to explain their strange stillness or the green fire of their feathers. Did I picture their former lives as "free of cares . . . protected from man by the jinn, given dominion over the fish" before the shot surprised them and they thought "it must be raining stones from the sky"?

The pleasures of these hunting poems are not dissimilar perhaps to the pleasures of hunting, as I imagine them—the freshness of the outdoors, the beauty of a cool morning, a satisfaction in hitting the target, the celebration of life through the ritual of death. What this book reminds me is that poetry is itself a hunt, a waking in darkness to set out into the materializing world and fit the pursuit to the quarry, matching words to sights and sounds, finding the right simile to pin down what is fleeting. And what is the appetite for this, for capturing the transient, but an alert hunger? The business of the poet, the translator, and the reader is, these poems seem to say, to stay in "yarak."

A. E. Stallings
University of Oxford

Introduction

A poetically gifted aesthete with no taste for politics; an ambitionless, pleasure-seeking son of a murdered caliph brought up by a doting and overprotective grandmother; a reluctant ruler who was forced to grasp the reins of power for just one day before he was discovered hiding in the home of a jeweler friend and executed on the spot, Abū l-ʿAbbās ʿAbd Allāh ibn al-Muʿtazz cuts a tragic, if somewhat ludicrous, figure in the annals of the Abbasid caliphate.[1]

Such, at least, was the image of Ibn al-Muʿtazz current in scholarship for much of the twentieth century. If history is written by the victor, then the vanquished Ibn al-Muʿtazz existed after his death simply as the author of several works on poetics and etiquette, and a diwan of poetry: preserved, like so many diwans, decontextualized, like a display in a cabinet of curiosities. However, this tragedy of Ibn al-Muʿtazz the reluctant caliph hinges on an impoverished notion of political activity and on an equally impoverished notion of the role of poetry in elite Abbasid circles of the third/ninth century. His image as the tragic aesthete is not a modern invention: it is the picture of him painted in a number of classical sources. But some sources do position him more solidly in a sociopolitical context. We must consider, therefore, how accurate the tragic image is, and how we approach, in a historically informed manner, a body of occasional poetry that has lost any connection with the occasions that caused it to be composed.

Life

Ibn al-Muʿtazz, the direct descendant of six caliphs, was born on 23 Shaban 247/1 November 861 in Samarra, in the palace complex built to house the Turkish troops on which the caliphate relied so heavily—the very troops who in 247/861 had assassinated his grandfather, the caliph al-Mutawakkil. His father, Abū Muḥammad Aḥmad ibn Jaʿfar, ascended to the caliphate with the regnal title al-Muʿtazz ("He Whose Might Comes from God") in 252/866. He had been imprisoned by his predecessor, his cousin al-Mustaʿīn (r. 248–52/862–66), but eventually the latter lost his power struggle with the praetorian Turks during the period often referred to as "the Samarran anarchy." In 255/869 al-Muʿtazz, unable to pay the military, was deposed and imprisoned, where he was either killed or starved to death. Ibn al-Muʿtazz's grandmother, the concubine Qabīḥah (whose name, "Ugly," is clearly euphemistic and apotropaic), assumed care of the young prince and arranged for his education. He was put under the tutelage of Aḥmad ibn Ṣaʿīd al-Dimashqī (d. 307/919) and received instruction from the leading language experts al-Mubarrad (d. 286/900) and Thaʿlab (d. 291/904).

The new caliph, al-Muhtadī (r. 255–56/869–70), the son of Caliph al-Wāthiq (r. 272–32/842–47), removed Ibn al-Muʿtazz and his grandmother Qabīḥah, together with several other senior Abbasids, from the center of power in Iraq to Mecca, in an attempt to consolidate power in his branch of the Abbasid family and to control potential rival claimants to the caliphate. When al-Muʿtaḍid came to power (r. 278–89/891–902), he invited Ibn al-Muʿtazz to move to Baghdad, once again the seat of the caliphate. Ibn al-Muʿtazz declared his fealty to the caliph by composing a long poem celebrating the caliph's exploits and by writing a work on the courtly etiquette of wine drinking, a work that celebrated the justness of his reign. With al-Muʿtaḍid's death, however, Ibn al-Muʿtazz was once again incarcerated until the oath of allegiance could be sworn to the new caliph, al-Muktafī (r. 289–95/902–8). Turmoil erupted upon al-Muktafī's death as the various factions at the court schemed to put a replacement upon the throne. One of al-Muktafī's brothers, Jaʿfar, was installed as caliph with the title al-Muqtadir (r. 295–320/908–32), but there was a powerful faction behind Ibn al-Muʿtazz, and on 20 Rabi al-Awwal 296/17 December 908 they declared Ibn al-Muʿtazz caliph. The palace guards were, however, partisans of al-Muqtadir, and Ibn al-Muʿtazz, abandoned by his supporters, was strangled later that day.

Ibn al-Muʿtazz was obviously an attractive candidate for the caliphate by virtue of his birth alone, and some sources describe him as well acquainted with the intricacies of governance and the political life. Unlike many of his relatives in the Abbasid dynasty, however, he seems not to have resorted to bloodthirsty means in the scramble for power, but to have cultivated a sophisticated and urbane persona and to have based his fitness to rule on, among other things, his reputation for wisdom and learning. If Ibn al-Muʿtazz had not been such an accomplished and prolific poet, and if he had not composed works on literary theory and literary history, he would have joined the historical roster of Abbasid elite politicians and contenders for the caliphate who jockeyed for power and lost during the so-called Samarran anarchy.

Works

Ibn al-Muʿtazz's works are manifestly literary: they deal principally with poetics and literary history, and therefore at first blush seem (especially his poetry) to be devoid of political ambition or consequence. One of his earliest extant prose works is the seminal and hugely influential treatise on poetics, *The New Style* (*Kitāb al-Badīʿ*), partly composed before 273/886–87.[2] It is a work devoted to a discussion of the stylistic characteristics and rhetorical techniques in the poetry composed in the Abbasid empire from the last quarter of the second/eighth century onward by poets known generally as "Modernists" (*muḥdathūn*), a group to which Ibn al-Muʿtazz belonged. In the treatise, Ibn al-Muʿtazz's aim is to demonstrate that in fact such techniques and tropes are already in use in the Qur'an,

Hadith, early Arabic poetry (especially that of the Jahiliya), and in the speech of the Bedouin. The treatise thus belongs to a plethora of texts of the late third/ninth century in which autochthonous Arabian origins were posited for phenomena prized in Abbasid culture. This was especially important as several non-Arab interest groups regarded things Arab as inferior to Sassanian learning or Greek philosophy and science. This challenge resulted in what is sometimes referred to as the *shuʿūbiyyah* controversy.

Two features of Ibn al-Muʿtazz's stance in *The New Style* are significant. Ibn al-Muʿtazz was a member of a neo-Ḥanbalī elite that eschewed the radical populism typical of the Ḥanbalī movement in Baghdad in favor of a sophisticated syncretism, which revered the Qurʾan and Prophetic Sunna as its religious and intellectual foundations, while remaining open to Sassanian-inspired courtly practices and ethos. The book thus seeks to anchor the "novel" (*badīʿ*) style in earlier textual bases, principal among which is the Qurʾan. Moreover, as poetry was the supreme artistic and aesthetic value system prevalent among the elite, Ibn al-Muʿtazz, as a prince of the dynasty, was seeking to establish his personal Abbasid authority over literary patrimony and poetic creativity, as he expanded the textual authorities recognized by his contemporaries to encompass "Modernist" poetry and not simply the genius of the ancients of the Jahiliya.

A similar tendency is discernible in his survey *Modernist Poets Who Have Praised Caliphs and Viziers, Arranged by Rank* (*Ṭabaqāt al-shuʿarāʾ al-muḥdathīn fī madḥ al-khulafāʾ wa-l-wuzarāʾ*), a treatise that opens with a declaration of Ibn al-Muʿtazz's aristocratic pedigree and of the princely right to rule. The introduction to the book may reveal the presence of a hagiographer's or forger's hand, but the sentiment is clear enough—the author's program is to single out for attention those poets who have celebrated the achievements of the ruling dynasty and its servants. The work is also resolutely anti-Shiʿi in its bias.

Another work combining Abbasid courtly culture, the elite ethos, and neo-Ḥanbalī syncretism is *Images to Bring Joy* (*Fuṣūl al-tamāthīl fī tabāshīr al-surūr*), a study of bacchanalia and courtly etiquette. In the courtly rituals surrounding the consumption of alcohol, the Abbasid elite had followed in the footsteps of the Sassanians. Ibn al-Muʿtazz was himself al-Muʿtaḍid's intimate table companion (*nadīm*), a position of high trust and esteem. Ibn al-Muʿtazz's syncretism is evident in this work, as is his tendency to bemoan the degeneracy of the times (known in Arabic as *dhamm al-zamān*). The difference here is that he does not lambast the current age but the recent past that has been tarnished by the denigration of the nobility. For Ibn al-Muʿtazz, al-Muʿtaḍid's reign heralds the restitution of the rightful social order.

A similar stance with regard to the ills of society is discernible in Ibn al-Muʿtazz's *Apothegms* (*Kitāb al-Ādāb*), possibly the same work as his *Brief Statements* (*Fuṣūl qiṣār*), which is no longer extant in its original form. *Apothegms* is a loosely articulated miscellany of wisdom lore drawn from Late Antique, Sassanian, and Arab traditions. Abbasid courtly society loved a witticism, a sententious well-turned phrase, and it was one of the mechanisms whereby men of authority established and upheld their worldly experience and fitness to hold the positions they occupied. These utterances also functioned as rallying points for followers and the like-minded: gnomic foci that contributed to an esprit de corps or forged a communal, even sectarian, identity. The prime example of this over the centuries is the reverence shown to the rhetorical genius of the fourth caliph, ʿAlī ibn Abī Ṭālib (r. 35–40/656–61), be it in collections of his wise sayings or in al-Sharīf al-Raḍī's (d. 406/1015) *Paragon of Eloquence* (*Nahj al-balāghah*), a florilegium of the speeches of ʿAlī.

Verse

Poetry was one of the means whereby the learned members of third/ninth century society communicated with each other and maintained networks of patronage, friendship, and loyalty. When the poet happens to be a prince of the realm, and a candidate for the caliphate, such networks are bound to be closely imbricated in the dynamics of power. Much of Ibn al-Muʿtazz's diwan, therefore, is devoted to vaunts, eulogies, reproaches, exhortations, worldly wisdom, and congratulations. Many of his poems describe the pleasures of the symposiac lifestyle, a lifestyle of crucial significance for the upper echelons of courtly society, occasions when allegiances and friendships were nurtured.

Ibn al-Muʿtazz's *Ṭardiyyāt,* his hunting poems, to which this volume is devoted, are no exception. These poems describe expeditions to course for game with saluki hounds, or to hunt quarry with raptors, or to shoot with the pellet bow. Invariably, the hunting expedition began in the dead of night, proceeded to an early-morning hunt before the sun was too high in the sky, and ended with a feast in which the game was cooked and shared and accompanied by a drinking session. Many of the poems included here would have been composed or declaimed during these festivities at the conclusion of the hunt. As al-Shabushtī's (d. ca. 388/988) *Book of Monasteries* (*Kitāb al-Diyārāt*) amply demonstrates, most hunting expeditions took place in the grounds of Iraq's Christian monasteries, where the hunting party could have easy access to wine and its associated pleasures.[3]

Poems 37 and 55 remind us that hunting was not a discrete pursuit but was an inflection of the apparatus of rulership. In the formal terms of Arabic poetry, Poem 55 is a tripartite qasida (composed in *sarīʿ* meter). Its three parts are an amatory section with the abandoned campsite motif (*nasīb* with *dhikr al-aṭlāl*), the vaunt (*fakhr*), and the hunting scene (*ṭardiyyah*). This is not an unusual combination of themes and is not too dissimilar from the most famous poem in Arabic, the Suspended Ode (*Muʿallaqah*) of Imruʾ al-Qays, with its amatory boast, vaunt, hunt, and storm description. In Ibn al-Muʿtazz's poem, however, the first two themes are, in keeping with much "Modernist" (*muḥdath*) poetry, inverted: the poet rejects the value of lamenting the deserted campsites and the poet's infatuation with a love object (a gorgeous young man rather than a beautiful woman), and his boast is in fact a vituperation of the ancestral claims of a group whose identity is obscure but to whom he refers as "Nabataean farmers."

In terms of the internal logic of the first two themes of the poem, the shock, dismay, and outrage the poet feels on hearing the preposterous claims of the Nabataean farmers incite him to abandon any idea of indulging his emotions in weeping over love and time lost. What does this have to do with the goshawk hunt of the poem's third section? Internally, there are indications that the hunting scene of Poem 55 is not simply tacked on as an afterthought to the preceding lines: not only are the goshawks able to kill any quarry they hunt, but they also attack their prey like the militia when they grab hold of men's beards, and the goshawks are compared to "old men / who've seen how easily fortune can change." The poet speaks not only as a seasoned and capable hunter in complete control of fantastically, preternaturally endowed beasts but also as a man of authority, one presumably accustomed to commanding militia. The poem's final reference to the mutability of time is a thinly disguised warning, directed at the Nabataean farmers. In many cultures, including Abbasid culture, the royal hunt was a ceremonial celebration of the ruler's military prowess and fitness to rule. This hunting scene enlists those values in support of the admonition directed by the poet at the Nabataean farmers. Poem 55 thus becomes, in poetic terms, an example of the vaunt, which is expressed as a threat of attack. The effectiveness of the threat is expressed through the successful hunt.

Poem 37 is, in formal terms, a bipartite qasida (composed in *khafīf* meter). Its eighteen lines are divided into a hunting scene, in which the mounted poet chases down an onager jack, and several lines of apothegms (*ḥikmah*) with a distinctly ascetic (*zuhd*) stamp, in which the poet ponders "life's contradictions" and expresses his reliance on God's will. Unlike Poem 55, the two parts of the poem have little to do with each other in formal terms. It is almost as if a redactor had come across two distinct compositions that shared the same rhyme and meter and juxtaposed them. The poem as an entity only properly holds together if we consider it as an expression, a gesture, of

Ibn al-Muʿtazz's princely persona. The royal hunt, conducted unambiguously by the poet himself, and not via an intermediary such as a huntsman or a retainer, expresses both the prince's fitness to rule, as provider for his people, and his military prowess. To hunt an onager on horseback requires a horseman of skill: the onager, a hard-running creature, can attain speeds approaching forty miles (sixty-five kilometers) per hour. The apothegmatic lines declare the prince's sagacity and establish his worldly experience, qualities required of the just ruler. The poem in the form in which it has come down to us only makes sense if we consider it as voicing a political identity.

Poems 37 and 55 demonstrate that in Ibn al-Muʿtazz's world the hunt was not simply an elite pastime but a potent and resonant symbolic gesture of leadership. I think it plausible that both poems were declaimed at the conclusion of the hunting expeditions they describe—rallying cries around which the prince's comrades could muster and declare their allegiance.

Military prowess, wisdom, fitness to rule, and the comradeship of the hunt are inflections of a political demeanor that relies for its efficacy and appeal on a cult of heroic masculinity.

Heroic Masculinity and the Hunt

Hunting scenes occur in a liminal zone: they take place at dawn and are set in a pleasance—a secluded enclosure or garden, often inviolate, or, as Ibn al-Muʿtazz says, "protected from man by the jinn" (Poem 59). The hunt, however, does not function as a rite of initiation, for the skilled hunter takes center stage, and he is already an initiate. The hunt is an arena in which the hunter's heroic masculinity is put to the test. In this liminal space, the hunter must not only exercise all his skills of decision-making, coordinating the hunt team and controlling the nonhuman hunters, but in order to vanquish the quarry must penetrate the phenomenology of the nonhuman world, of both nonhuman hunter and prey. To do this, the hero must merge his consciousness with that of the nonhumans involved in the chase—in a sense, he must efface himself and be able at the end of the hunt to recover his self. Short of combat and warfare, this was the ultimate crucible for heroic masculinity.

There is a paradox in the essence of hunting as an enterprise. As a means of providing sustenance, hunting is costly, unreliable, and dangerous. In the third/ninth century there were easier means of providing food, be it from livestock or from the agricultural heartlands of Iraq. Despite the evidence of the poems, not all hunting expeditions would have been successful, and the expense of maintaining a hunting team of raptors, dogs, horses, and cheetahs must have been possible only for the wealthiest: presumably most elites would have participated in hunting expeditions without assuming the central role of the epic hunter. There would also at times have been considerable danger involved—for example, in a mounted horseman chasing an onager running at full speed.

Despite its dangers and costly inefficiency, hunting was popular with the Abbasid elites because of its symbolism. It functioned as the theater in which culture heroes such as Ibn al-Muʿtazz could put themselves on display and embody the values society and its regnal dynasty prized in its rulers: capability, prowess, decision-making, bravery, skill, and fortitude. It is the task of the culture hero to protect, disseminate, and at times enforce these values.

The communal feast of meat sharing that concluded a hunting expedition would, in terms of its symbolic capital, have been prized because the food was acquired after such an investment of labor and skill. It also was an occasion for the altruism and largesse of leadership. Hunting is thus a symbolic representation and enactment of fitness to rule, and its violence, inflicted on nonhumans, was thereby asserted over the enemies of the polity. The hunting poems of Ibn al-Muʿtazz celebrate and immortalize his royal status and prestige, and communicate his status as an embodiment of heroic masculinity.

The Homosocial World of the Ghazal

Of the Arabic poetic genres, the *ṭardiyyah* is semiotically closest in spirit to the love lyric (*ghazal*), and in particular those compositions in which the poet-lover is hunted and ensnared by the love object, male or female. In such pieces, the love object often features as a gazelle. The epic hunter, vanquisher of the nonhuman world, abjectly and voluntarily surrenders himself to the snares and charms of a young boy or girl. These deploy the traits typical of the quarry as it hunts down and destroys the hunter, who is then wounded by the very object of his heart's desire. Unlike the *ṭardiyyah*, which culminates in a successful kill, the *ghazal* terminates in failure: the love object is always out of reach and unattainable—and should that object be attained, it is quickly replaced by another unattainable object. The epic hunter of the *ṭardiyyah* is always a victim in the *ghazal*, his masculinity ever undone. However, the true hunter in the *ghazal* is not the love object, but the poet's own desire: his desire has no choice, invariably indulging in the chase and thus becoming a victim, enthusiastically embracing perpetual failure.

Three of Ibn al-Muʿtazz's *ṭardiyyāt*, Poems 30, 45, and 50, exemplify how the value system of masculinity, its prowess, mastery, and control, are subverted in the *ghazal*. Poem 45 is a reflection of days past, an evocation of a hare hunt with sakers and salukis that follows the customary *ṭardiyyah* pattern of early departure, the journey to the pleasance "through meadows awake with flowers," the description of nonhuman hunters, and the kill, followed by a communal feast. In this poem, however, no mention is made of the roast meats; instead, a drinking scene ensues in which the *sāqī*, the wine server, is a gazelle of a boy whose eyes bewitch the poet. The poem ends with the hunter-poet unable "to recover from one of his looks." The saker hunt of Poem 50 dispenses with the early departure and journey to the pleasance and concludes with a feasting scene in which the poet, "a lover beyond the pale of love," basks in "an admirer's devotion" as he quaffs his wine.

In a further set of variations on these themes, Poem 30 features a love object who is a deadly hunter described in vivid terms as a goshawk. The poem opens with the early-morning departure and journey to the pleasance through fields "of white and red and yellow jewels," and somewhat surprisingly jumps to the communal celebration without any mention of a nonhuman hunter or kill scene. In this radically recast *ṭardiyyah*, the poet includes the hunt scene with nonhuman hunter within the description of the symposium and its beguiling *sāqī*, "a languid-eyed gazelle," a master of "secret debauchery." This love object cum heroic hunter terrifies his prey with his splendid goshawk, which is a metaphor for his manhood, "poised on the red glove / her wings raised," ready to kill.

Poem 30 is one of the gems of this collection, a showcase of Ibn al-Muʿtazz at his most dazzling, and a reminder that the developed love poetry of the third/ninth century was an expression of homosocial desire, composed by men for an audience of other men and in competition with other men, about love objects both male and female, in order to create, foster, and participate in the public intimate—that communal space in which what are ostensibly private feelings are publicly celebrated and shared—and to cultivate a comportment of voyeurism. In this respect, *ṭardiyyah* and *ghazal* are the Janus faces of elite masculinity in the Abbasid era.

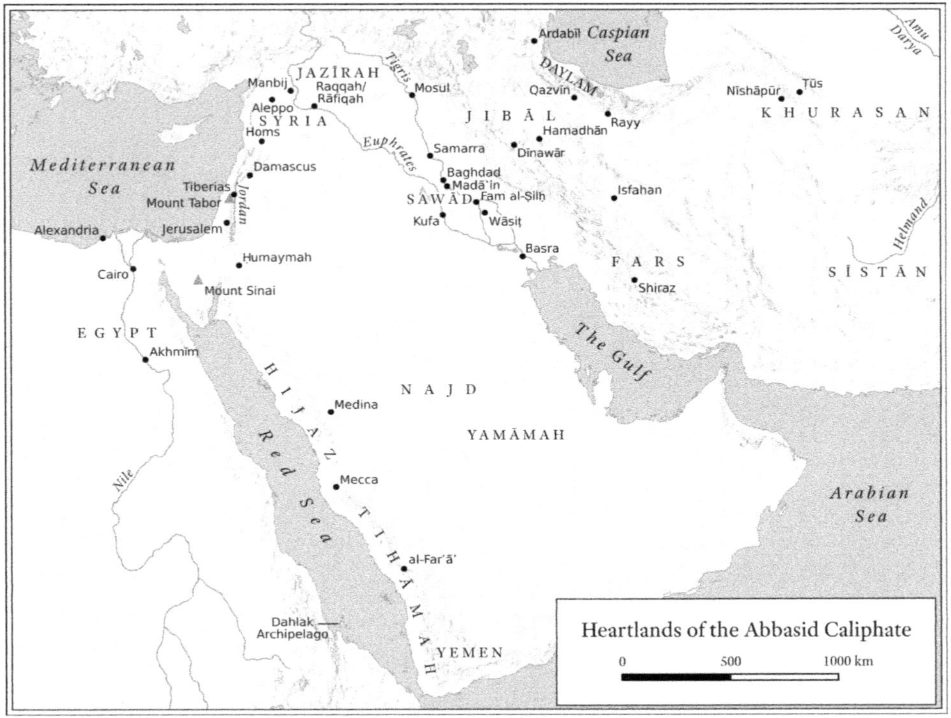
Heartlands of the Abbasid Caliphate
0
500
1000 km
Mediterranean Sea
Caspian Sea
The Gulf
Red Sea
Arabian Sea
Amu Darya
Tigris
Euphrates
Jordan
Nile
Helmand
JAZĪRAH
SYRIA
JIBĀL
DAYLAM
KHURASAN
SAWĀD
FARS
SĪSTĀN
EGYPT
HIJAZ
NAJD
YAMĀMAH
TIHĀMAH
YEMEN
Ardabīl
Manbij
Raqqah/
Rāfiqah
Mosul
Qazvīn
Nīshāpūr
Tūs
Aleppo
Homs
Rayy
Hamadhān
Samarra
Dīnawār
Damascus
Baghdad
Madā'in
Fam al-Ṣilḥ
Isfahan
Tiberias
Mount Tabor
Jerusalem
Alexandria
Kufa
Wāsiṭ
Basra
Humaymah
Shiraz
Cairo
Mount Sinai
Akhmīm
Medina
Mecca
al-Far'ā'
Dahlak
Archipelago

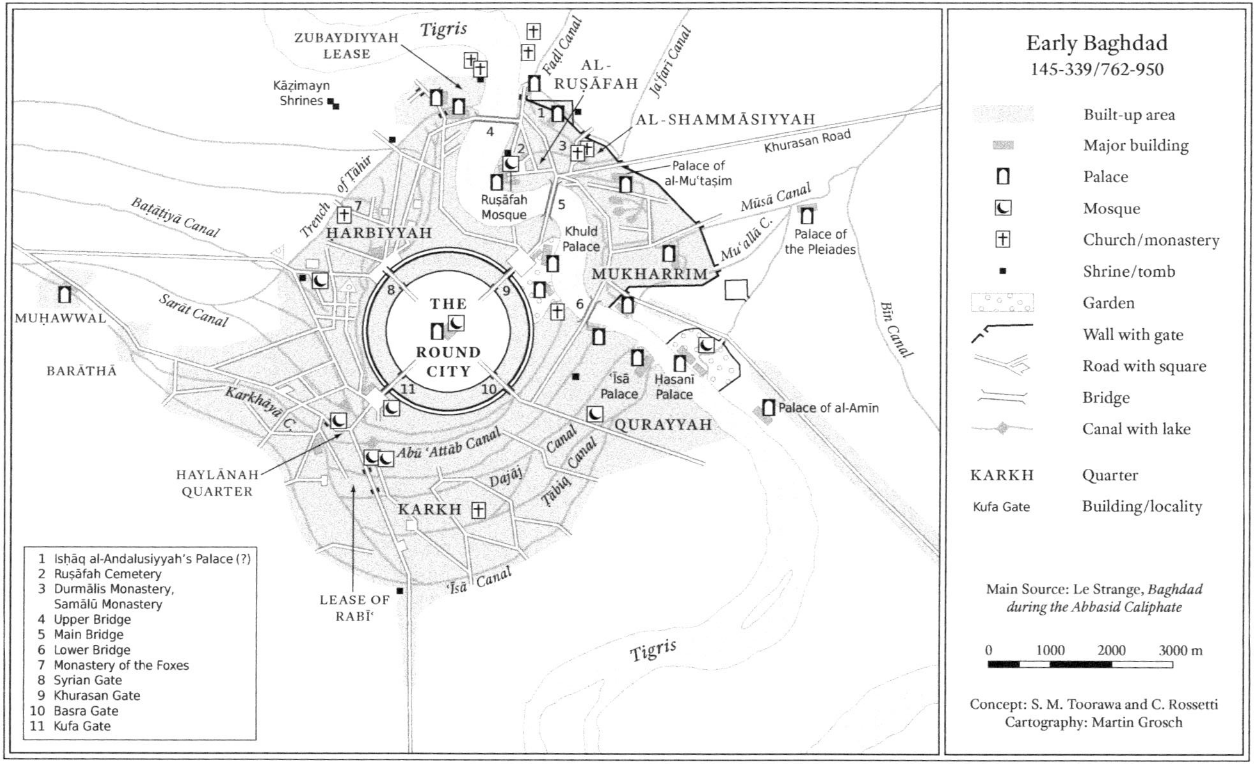
Early Baghdad
145-339/762-950
Built-up area
Major building
Palace
Mosque
Church/monastery
Shrine/tomb
Garden
Wall with gate
Road with square
Bridge
Canal with lake
KARKH Quarter
Kufa Gate Building/locality
Main Source: Le Strange, *Baghdad during the Abbasid Caliphate*
0 1000 2000 3000 m
Concept: S. M. Toorawa and C. Rossetti
Cartography: Martin Grosch
Tigris
ZUBAYDIYYAH LEASE
Kāẓimayn Shrines
Faḍl Canal
AL-RUṢĀFAH
Jaʿfarī Canal
AL-SHAMMĀSIYYAH
Khurasan Road
Palace of al-Muʿtaṣim
Ruṣāfah Mosque
Mūsā Canal
Muʿallā C.
Palace of the Pleiades
Khuld Palace
MUKHARRIM
Bīn Canal
Trench of Ṭāhir
Baṭāṭiyā Canal
HARBIYYAH
THE ROUND CITY
Sarāt Canal
MUḤAWWAL
BARĀTHĀ
ʿĪsā Palace
Ḥasanī Palace
Palace of al-Amīn
Karkhāyā C.
QURAYYAH
Abū ʿAttāb Canal
Canal
Dajāj
Ṭābiq Canal
HAYLĀNAH QUARTER
KARKH
ʿĪsā Canal
LEASE OF RABĪʿ
Tigris
1 Isḥāq al-Andalusiyyah's Palace (?)
2 Ruṣāfah Cemetery
3 Durmālis Monastery, Samālū Monastery
4 Upper Bridge
5 Main Bridge
6 Lower Bridge
7 Monastery of the Foxes
8 Syrian Gate
9 Khurasan Gate
10 Basra Gate
11 Kufa Gate

Note on the Translation

Throughout this project, my aim as translator has been clarity, be it of diction, image, or episode. There is an immediacy to Ibn al-Muʿtazz's *Ṭardiyyāt* that I have striven to highlight in English. I hope the result is that his miniatures are as striking in English as they are in Arabic.

The style of the mature tradition of the *ṭardiyyah* that Ibn al-Muʿtazz's poems represent is concise, often pointillist. There are few wasted words. His primary stylistic technique is parataxis. Episodes, descriptions, and similes follow one another, usually with only an implicit transition. The pattern of the hunt (early-morning departure, description of nonhuman hunter, chase and kill, and feast) provides the narrative structure for many of the poems, a sequence that also often remains implicit in the poem. In my translations, I have decided to make that sequence visible, to bring it to the surface, with a view to making the dramatic structure of each poem recognizable to the reader new to the material.

The art of falconry and hawking boasts a developed and sophisticated vocabulary in English. I have dipped into its lexical riches to capture features and behaviors of the raptors as described by Ibn al-Muʿtazz. I have included these terms in the Glossary.

In two poems (51 and 52), I decided to render some nonhuman epithets as names. We rarely encounter nonhumans with names in the genre, an indication perhaps of their mythic presence (for it is unlikely that owners and trainers would *not* have named the nonhumans), but it seemed appropriate to render the adjectives like this on these occurrences.

I have added titles to the poems and have tried to complete this book without any endnotes: my ideal is an English translation of an Arabic text that does not require the portentous and intrusive freight of the scholarly note. I have not quite succeeded, of course. I suppose I would be a character created by Borges for one of his *Ficciones* if I had.

Notes to the Introduction

1 This introduction relies heavily on Julia Bray, "Ibn al-Muʿtazz and Politics: The Question of the Fuṣūl Qiṣār," and Wolfhart Heinrichs, "Ibn al-Muʿtazz (1 November 861–17 December 908)." I have learned much from Catherine Bates, *Masculinity and the Hunt: Wyatt to Spenser*. In Further Reading, I list other works that have informed my thinking on Ibn al-Muʿtazz, his poetry, and his world. For more information on the role of hunting in the pre-Islamic and Islamic imaginary, see my introduction to *Fate the Hunter: Early Arabic Hunting Poems*.

2 A new edition and translation by Huda Fakhreddine is in preparation for the Library of Arabic Literature.

3 Al-Shabushtī, *The Book of Monasteries*, edited and translated by Hilary Kilpatrick.

In Deadly Embrace

Like White Teeth on Red Lips

A description of a dog:

Like white teeth on red lips
dawn shone naked on the horizon,
and as the night star went into hiding,
darkness grew old, its hair flecked.

To the spring where oryx and gazelles live
we brought death, this fearsome bitch,
her tail raised like a brown scorpion's,
her loins arched, trained and lean,
like a cloak's fringe or a black *maddah*
sketched by a reed pen.
Carried on wings of air, quicker
than the blink of an eye, our bitch
steals her steps like a lame camel
on hot sand.
The bitch's partner
is lean and sleek, vaunted for his bright
white coat. With muscles taut,
he's like sky dust shed by a shooting star.
He knows the calls—when to hold back,
when to attack, his long ears like the petals
of dark irises flopping on his flanks,
his nails as sharp as a cobbler's awl,
his eyes clear, dust-free, raindrop-pure.

Alert to the call, he glides
across the dunes like a spangled snake,
spotting a herd grazing with their fawns,
where plain and upland meet in a distant field
aflame with wildflowers, hidden from foragers
and scouts, green as a dark snake's belly,
fed gifts of cold dew at dusk and dawn
as the breezes sigh, sloughed skins strewn
about, like a hag's flecked braids of hair.

Before tiring, he hunted down fifty victims,
drinking their blood,
leaving their flesh untouched.

What a Waste!

About an incompetent archer:

> Hope defeated by despair!
> You fired an earthen pellet
> into the sky and hit fresh air.
> What a waste!
> Good hunting, water carrier!

Like a Slice of Air

Gemini set in the sky
and dawn erased the night.
Quicker than a blink,
like a slice of air,
she spotted a herd
in a lush green field
hidden by the dew-
fed foliage.
Effortless in her slaughter,
she seemed from afar
like a black *maddah*
drawn by a stylus,
exchanging flesh for blood.

The Heavy Beat of Thunder

The rain drummed the heavy beat
of thunder from a cloud,
insides brimming with light and water.
The stars quenched the thirsty soil.
Night fell after the first shower
and lightning lit up the cloud,
its face smeared in pitch as it released
its load of rain, draining its eyes of tears,
its death giving birth
to blossoms in a fertile plain,
where moisture lay hidden, ready
to burst into life, and where I
arrived in a shroud of darkness.

Like a River in Spate

A description of a horse:

> Who will trade my gray hair
> for locks black as grapes?
> Who will halt its attack
> on my lustrous head and beard,
> on my quick-beating heart?
> Where are the ravishing girls,
> where the folly of youth
> with its excesses
> so easily excused?
>   Gone.
> Vanished. Now far away.
>
> I crossed the dark on a young
> branded thoroughbred,
> moving like a river in spate,
> scattering the rocks on the road
> with hooves like goblets overturned,
> his blaze smiling where his brow
> knit in a frown. He chased his quarry,
> legs kicking up a dust storm—
> before it settled, blood was shed.

In Youth's Full Flush

A description of a tiercel:

> Dawn showed her teeth,
> laughing at the night
> like an African slave fleeing his owners.
> I crossed the dark with a tiercel
> in youth's full flush, no higher praise—
> chest as if clad in a viper's sloughed skin,
> talons tightly fitted to spear shafts
> dyed wet on the day of the hunt.
> Even our gos isn't this good a hunter—
> we're glad we brought him and not her.
> Our elation spurs him to fly ever faster—
> decorated with patterned letters
> you won't find in any book,
> he's swifter than our gos,
> flying to exact a blood oath.
> On early forays he can be relied on,
> responding after only one call.
> If he met Death, he'd know no fear.

Like a Desert Snake

With her coat of gold,
she scorns other dogs,
gliding like a desert snake,
her eyes meteor-bright.

She Rides the Wind

Wrapped in a crow's wings,
night, its youthful hair unflecked,
was as black as a jilbab.

A saluki bitch, meteor-bright.
Out of the blocks she explodes
like a blazing star on its course,
with a light tread, victory in her nails
and teeth, eyes fixed on the prize.

As dawn removes her niqab,
gleaming like a blade visible
through its sheath, our bitch
spots herds of gazelles
grazing. Trained, eager
for the chase, she rides the wind
in her stride, faster than an arrow
in flight.
                She runs down ten deer
in a row, patiently waiting for us
to catch up, no blood on her teeth.

The Veil of the Unseen

A description of a gos:

I left early to hunt with noble comrades,
armed with a superb gos, sure to catch game.
For the birds squawking in the canal,
it's a close encounter with Death
and time to pay our hawk their soul debt.
Like gold nails hammered into her head
her eyes pierce the veil of the unseen.
She did not disappoint.
                                        Sitting high
on the left hand, like a stiff-backed emir
dispensing gifts, her beak was a blood-dyed
spearhead, her plump train feathers
draped over cotton tufts. She stood tall,
arms wrapped in fringed linen breeches.
She spotted prey, blinked,
then moved—and, trusting her quest,
the troop unsheathed their knives.

God's Scourge

A description of a saker and a horse:

Dawn was a shock of gray hair.
I crossed the dark on a branded horse
in his prime, like a river in spate,
ears like date-heavy palm leaves
or myrtle bunched on a twig,
with a tail like the fronds of a lazy
cloud, or a cypress in lush soil,
his hooves kohl-black like a foot
swollen with venom,
or a goblet turned upside down,
faster than a blink of the eye,
or water spilling from a jug,
or thoughts flashing in the mind,
or a sly, furtive look—he's a bright
ball of fire-spitting flame.

On a skilled falconer's glove
I brought a saker in yarak,
trained to perfection.
Quicker than a stolen glance,
she rained down God's scourge,
like the crack of a whip.[1]
She squinted, grimaced, rolled
her mute eye so keen
it does away with distance—

then stooped
like water down a well.

Spotting some geese in a pond,
she jumped, as if spooked,
in pursuit of her desire.
Let her quarry range far—
when she flies, north or south,
there will be blood.

A Squint-Eyed Grimace

A saker in yarak, well-trained,
keen eyes that see for miles,
stooping like a bucket
falling down an old well.
With a roll of her mute eye,
like a squint-eyed grimace,
she spots geese in a pond
and shoots north and south
as if scared out of her wits.

A Gown of Jade and Gold

A description of a female cheetah:

The best way to hunt is a cheetah
that flies on four legs
thin as whip thongs,
pouncing and clutching prey
to her chest like a woman
clasping a man in unrequited love.
When the prey sees her chase,
its soul whispers, "Death is here."
She sits in her pillion, like a Turkish beauty
captured by Arabs, kohl from her eyes
smeared on her cheeks, dressed
in a dazzling gown of jade and gold.

We spent the day roasting gazelle
meat on the coals, and greedily
swallowing it barely cooked.

Like a Patterned Snake

A description of dogs:

> Crow-black night was curtained off,
> behind locked doors. Dawn removed
> her hijab, like a shock of gray
> on a young head. I crossed the dark
> with a swiftly pouncing bitch, like a star
> violently exploding on the horizon,
> gliding like a patterned snake, eyes
> meteor-bright, never wrong.
>
> Her jaws snapped the necks
> of so many desert hares,
> pinning them in her grip—
> no blood was shed by her teeth,
> as she saved them for her handlers
> who lagged behind.

A Glint of Sword

A description of a dog:

Dawn appeared in her hijab
like a glint of sword in sheath.

I left early with my comrades
to hunt with a haughty bitch,
swifter than a furtive glance,
gliding like a patterned snake,
eyes meteor-bright, never wrong.

Her teeth snapped the necks
of so many desert hares,
pinning them in her grip,
saving them for her handlers,
but without a drop of blood.

Meteor-Bright

A description of a bitch:

> A bitch, meteor-bright.
> Look—out of the blocks,
> her tread so light
> you'd think she was a star
> exploding in the night.

A Babel of Language

A description of traps, bird-lime sticks, and nets:

What hunts but does not move?
What rides but does not budge?
What is ignoble and stands
on a minbar but does not preach?
What food remains in the desert
and brings life face to face with death?
What is a prison where the captives
are fettered and a babel of language
by every nation can be heard?

What spear inflicts no wounds,
draws no blood, is used
for neither chase nor raid,
and is dyed not with warriors'
blood but with Death's saliva?
What lets nothing escape,
clinging to breast and chest,
a jail dangling from the thongs
tied to the spearheads
fitted to unburnished spears
made from quills stripped of feathers?
Mounted high on their hafts,
you'd think they were rats' tails
turned upside down.

A Love of Death

A description of a sparrow hawk:

> A sparrow hawk that satisfies
> everything my hand desires.
> His hunt will never fail:
> no fleet quarry can outrun him.
> When cast, he flies like an arrow
> that never misses. Well-drilled,
> responsive to the call, his only flaw
> a love of death!

Hungry, Dawn to Dusk

A description of salukis:

> I sing of a prancer, a ferocious,
> malicious tormenter of oryx,
> at the head of three lean-hipped salukis,
> hungry dawn to dusk. He lunges
> at four fleet cows, as if trying to catch
> pearls slipping from a necklace.

In Battle Gear

A description of a goshawk and a horse:

Morning drove off the night
wrapped in its cloak of gloom,
as the Pleiades, sparked by a dawn burst,
blazed like torch fires and Gemini
died away in the sunrise,
fluttering on the horizon
like a flag in the wind.
                                        I startled the oryx,
mounted on a well-drilled, speedy charger,
tufts of hair at his hooves, his back
and withers tightly welded,
wading through water that reached
no higher than his white pasterns,
as if a girl in a red jilbab had fastened
a bracelet on her wrist: his blaze
was white as the early sun; his ribs
like the frame of a camel's litter,
fused to his spine whose vertebrae
were like the dense knot of a *khaṭṭī* spear;
his hooves, blue as turquoise and big
as boulders, peeled back the surface
of the ground; his feet, bold, lesion-free,
pounded the high roads with loud thuds,
like polo mallets, raising a dust storm
like a cloud of *ʿarfaj* smoke

or teased cotton tossed in the air.
Accompanied by a fine gos in battle gear,
her head dusty white, like a king
wearing a crown, her restless eyes,
keen and true, under white brows,
her eyelids like the cloth
of a litter-bearing camel,
her talons like thin, arched eyebrows,
her dappled feathers under black wings
patterned like a regal mantle.

We enjoyed a day of pleasure.
Some slaughtered the birds,
others kindled the fires,
some cooked the meat till it was done,
others, too impatient to wait,
swallowed it raw.

To Seize the Souls

A description of a gos:

> In the dark, just before dawn,
> with her silver body and jet-black
> coat of mail, she was like the general
> of an invincible army on the march
> to seize the souls of the living.

A Death Knell

A description of a gos:

> In the breath of dawn, I crossed the dark
> with a twitchy gos greedy for the kill.
> Eyes fixed on distant shapes, she beat
> the air with wings loud as the thud
> of the hooves of a champion stallion.
> She was dressed in fine feather mail,
> dappled as if with bubbles of wine,
> her bell chirruping like a hopper—
> a death knell to the collared and girdled birds
> afloat in the lake's eddies and pools.

Like a Bright Page

A description of a gos:

Picture the gos as the proud general
of a Persian army, a lavish leader—
he's the reason his people live at ease.
Her surprise attack brought terror,
subduing the abject birds, harrying them
to the water, delivering her verdict
from a perfumed beak and blood-
drenched talons. The birds screeched,
praying to be saved from her brutal clutches.
After a farsakh, when the sun stood proud
and grim night had fled, the gos glinted
like a bright page flecked with tiny script.

Tongues Like Daggers

A description of dogs:

> Our riders left early to meet at the cloister.
> The houndman brought thin salukis,
> prime, long under his care, well-trained,
> daughters of the wind, begging to run,
> urged on faster and faster, tongues
> hanging from mouths like daggers
> that slice through their sheaths.
> They held their prey in their paws
> without shedding a drop of blood—
> like young mothers suckling their babies.

In Rusty Hauberks

A description of a gos:

Night stretched across the land,
dawn's light uncertain.
The bold comrades stole an early march,
the hawks sitting tall on their arms
like generals clad in rusty hauberks.

A Watchful Demon

A description of dogs:

> Night lay gentle on the face of the earth,
> the cloak of the breeze moist and cold
> while dawn sparked in the murk.
> I crossed the dark with my drop-eared dogs,
> thin as leather leashes, whirlwinds
> homing in on their target, runners
> giving their all to the race, legs and feet
> fulfilling their promise. Our horsemen
> charged to the hunt. With the thud
> of the hooves, the ground burst into a storm
> of thunder and lightning, a watchful demon
> popped up then hid, a dust cloud rose
> and hung suspended in the sky
> like striped sheets drying on a line.
> The dogs split up on the plain,
> then charged in a file on the stony ground,
> covering a vast distance as if it were a small step.

Like an Arrow

A bitch too fast to be seen sprinting
once sicced from the leash.
I waded through a darkness
as black as her hide: my eyes
thought night had borrowed her coat.
She spotted ten animals who showed up
after I'd arrived. Unleashed,
she flew like an arrow from a bow.
Her greatest asset, how hard she worked—
Merciful God made me feel the pain
of her loss when she died.

An Inflamed Eye

A description of horses:

> The western horizon turned as red
> as the lid of an inflamed eye.
> The horses reached water in the dark.

AMOROUS APPROACHES

A description of cheetahs:

> I sing of identical cheetahs
> pared like fletched arrows, lean-
> bellied, sharpened to a fine point
> by long-distance runs, chasing *ẓaby*s
> who spurn their amorous approaches,
> as they cut across the dips and desert
> hollows like arrows sped by bows—
> I'm unable to tell which is quicker!

Astride the Glove

A description of a gos:

> I left before dawn, just as day broke,
> still wrapped in the jilbab
> night had buttoned over us, black as pitch
> like the skin of a naked Nubian.
> Night knew it was time for the hunt
> to shed blood, and morning restored
> our sight. Into the lists rode a knight
> astride the glove, standing tall
> like the lieutenant of a Persian squadron,
> alert to distant shapes; with mail
> like streaked marble or striated parchment,
> eyes as yellow as dinars, lids
> like the fringes of a Christian's belt,
> and talons like curved nails.
> She spotted birds in a creek
> with clear banks, where the water
> gurgled and the waves plashed
> as they swam through the frothing swell,
> chirping at nightfall, whistling
> like a fife band, with dark collars
> and beaks like half plectrums
> whittled by their maker.
> Before she grew vexed and wearied,
> our gos killed fifty birds,

snatching them with her talons
like a brutal tyrant who in victory
takes revenge on his victims,
his sword decreeing life or death.
Like a jet of fire, she felled her prey.

Scented with Ambergris

A description of a gos:

We crossed the dark on well-trained coursers
as dawn, like the blaze on a roan colt,
flitted on the fringes of night and the beasts rested
peacefully in their dens. The face of the earth
looked like a striped Yemeni cloak, or embroidery,
or white and red and yellow jewels,
and to my mind's eye its saplings,
with their eyes shut, seemed like mouths closed,
blossoms about to burst into flower,
half-smiles, with no teeth flashing.
The teardrop pools were clear of mud,
the leas, washed by a rain-soaked night,
resembled dirhams or tens
of verses of a Qur'an outspread.
The sun illumined the dark sky
like a tear welling in the corner of an eye.

We quaffed a strong wine, a heady vintage
that blazes like a bright lamp, poured,
cup by cup, from the hand of a languid-eyed gazelle,
his fringe scented with ambergris.
His lips parted to reveal toothsome jewels,
his plump buttocks swelled his gown
below the waist, his eyes spoke
of secret debauchery. He could teach

the innocent how to sin, terrifying his prey
with a dusty-white gos, as if clad
in a hasped coat of mail, her eyes burning
in their sockets, a beak with a dagger-sharp tip
you'd think was daubed with safflower,
a crown like a round boulder, mail decorated
in patterns like faint letters
on a parchment, a tail like a whetted blade
or like the curves of a peeled
date-palm spathe, a grip that splits
joints, with the power to break bones—
she sat poised on the red glove,
her wings raised like the sleeves of a busy man.

My Hair a Blaze of White

A description of dogs:

I yearn for the days of my youth
too soon gone—how I blossomed,
like a bud on a twig—how I long
for their intoxications and venial sins,
when our hearts were sprightly
and full of vim and all our hopes
opened before us. We lived
in the shade of an easy life
when Time did not yet sully joy
with anxiety or care.
Commanded by youth's deviltries,
I'd sally forth, a delight to houri-eyed girls.
Now, no longer worthy of envy,
my hair a blaze of white,
a new fate is mine.
Between the gloom of night
and the light heralding
dawn's arrival, I'd cross the dark
with my thin, slim-hipped dogs,
sprightly in collar and leash,
racing my steed's gallop
on the heels of startled game,
as I cried, "Bismillah!" and "Allahu akbar!,"
spelling death for the troop
of dark-eyed, long-necked oryxes

like crystal bowls of kohl,
our stallions' hooves pounding
like torrents on a stormy day,
kicking up cloud upon cloud
of battle murk, and shattering
rock after rock, pitting the face
of the earth with smallpox scars.

Black at Its Fringes

A description of the pellet bow:

The best way to hunt
is with a taut bowstring,
yellow, tightly twisted,
snorting when stroked
by the archer, its eye
weeping tears of clay
fashioned by a master fletcher
who with all his know-how
crafted them into balls
of identical shape, small pellets
more like pebbles than clay,
stored in navel-shaped pouches,
flying like sparks at hearts
and breasts.
Night was still black
at its fringes as we crossed
the dark to meet the dawn,
patiently taking up our position.
Light spread through the sky.
They came in droves, swimming,
on their way, with Fate's leave,
to a new meadow or river,
anxious eyes alert to danger—
an archer hurriedly fastened
string to bow and acted

decisively. His shots scattered
the flock. He wore out the lath,
almost ruining it. Birds fell
from the sky, some screaming
in danger, others stranded
on broken wing. Hubris
took control of the archer,
who exulted in his triumph
though he needed to be prudent.
The shooting continued in earnest
and the birds cried, "Humans never fire
pellets like this—it must be raining
stones from the sky!"

On the Crest of a Hill

A description of a saker and geese:

> She saw them when we were
> on the crest of a hill
> and flapped her wings
> like the wrist flick of a spear.
> Through stringy dust clouds
> she flew at bolt.
> She mantled—gripped,
> pecked, sliced, scooped
> treasures from skulls.

Vainglorious

A description of a cheetah:

> As the meadows breathed in the black
> of night, before things got early,
> before day stood up and sat down,
> before the Pleiades shone firebrand-
> bright, I crossed the edge of the dark
> with a cheetah trained to pounce
> upon its prey, whose lungs
> are like a smith's bellows,
> and who, taut as a twisted rope,
> sits motionless, like an excellent passenger,
> on the horse's back, eyes free of dust.
> Haughty, vainglorious, clad
> in everlasting symbols,
> like a yellow divining arrow
> shaken, then cast.
> Set free and sicced on his prey,
> he crouched low and took cover,
> outwitting his cautious quarry,
> master of opportune strikes.
> In the hunt, he comes into sight
> only when cornering his prey.

Kennel-Bred

A description of dogs:

> At dawn I crossed the dense dark
> with a fleet scent hound, kennel-
> bred and trained; its inquisitive nose
> sniffs the ground for signs of life;
> it plucks the timid hare from its set
> as you would a gray hair
> with your tweezers; the bane
> of bird and beast, this dog swarms
> like a locust, a hungry brute,
> thirsty only for the taste of blood
> in the hunt, never used in dogfights.

Flash Floods

A description of goshawks and dogs:

Come, comrade, get up! It's time to go
oryx hunting with our rapacious
hawks, dappled with embroidered
dots, and let's take our lean and swift
scent hounds, masters at sniffing out prey
and flushing it from the ground,
mighty warriors all, awaiting our permission
to tear apart the game. Let's bring a horse,
strong as flash floods, galloping up a storm.

He saw daybreak march off into night
and got up with a smile on his cheery face
bright as a newly minted dinar,
swapping his soft bed for the saddle.
At first light, we emptied so many coverts
and nests! Under a night of watery-eyed stars,
in dew and misty rain, I drank a pure draft
of wine, and banished all cares.

Trained in the Arena

A description of a horse:

> Night would be wrapped in a gown
> and I'd ride at pace, mounted
> on a short-haired, easy-running
> thoroughbred, her front legs
> gifted with speed, her strides long
> and wide as she overtook her quarry,
> built like a mighty stone temple,
> muscles trained in the arena,
> a blaze shining through her forelock
> like a spadix in the midst of palm leaves.
> She jumped a group of onagers,
> courageous jennies, fleet, fat,
> and in foal, their wombs hiding fetuses
> like water bugs or baby rats,
> the harem led by a jack as sturdy
> as a hefty staff, a desert dweller
> braying from his lookout, spooked
> by any shape that moved. We drove
> a whirlwind against him, rewarding his throat
> and belly with repeated thrusts of our lance.
> He pounded the rocks, but my mare
> kicked in hard, as if it were a race
> on the open road.
>   We pitched our tent,
> the wind flapping its walls like a bird

with clipped wings, or a devoted nurse
dandling a child in her arms,
and we ate our fill of fresh meat,
drinking water from meadow pools
shining bright as silver coins.

My people, nothing can be done
about life's contradictions,
about fates too meager or too full,
about those who shirk or take more
than their due, about this corrupt world
where good is mixed with bad,
sweet with sour, where some eat
their fill and are never sated
while others go ever hungry,
where we are all ensnared
by delusions and nobody aspires
to the right path, a path difficult
and remote, yet made easy by God,
a path on which those who stay
lazily at home perish, while the bold
who venture forth cheat death.
Every soul has its destined path to God.

In a Saffron Robe

A description of a dog:

> I sing of a lean hound
> with well-fitted joints,
> clad in a saffron robe,
> who fills with many a hope
> the hungry hunter too poor
> to mend his shoes.

At Night's End

A description of a tiercel:

> I crossed the dark at night's end
> with my pride and joy, my tiercel.
> As I carried him on my wrist,
> he was keen to take off,
> now pulling, now relenting.
> Then, beating the air with his wings,
> he took to the sky, in a glimpse
> like a shooting star.
> For our troop he provided a feast
> of juicy meat before the sun
> had dyed the earth red.

Impulsive on the Leash

A description of dogs:

> The Pleiades lay low in the sky,
> the hair of fretful night turned
> gray. We drove the death-dealing dogs,
> impulsive on the leash, toward the tender-
> necked desert gazelles.
>   In the mirage-like
> dust cloud, it was as if they scooped up pearls
> fallen to the ground, and returned them
> to their earring hoops—salukis
> dancing with energy, raising their whip-
> like tails, ears thin as the teeth of a comb,
> their long arrowy muzzles fused
> to their spines; luminous as pearls
> locked away in a jewel box.

Brutal and Hard

A description of a saker:

Brutal and hard.
Blood shed
without warning.
What its eyes see
its talons take.

The Face of Fear

A description of a peregrine and a crow:

> It approached, hesitant, eyes
> on the alert, cautious. On the ground
> it looked like an odd boot pulled off
> in front of a large army,
> black as a rain cloud's shadow.
> In the meadow, carefree,
> it preened and pampered itself.
> But life is full of contradictions—
> often the same thing can be good and bad.
> It was shocked by a glimpse
> of the face of fear, then flew
> in a spurt till, beguiled by Time's
> wiles, it yielded. Death
> had arrived—an expert hunter,
> thwacking, binding to, tearing
> the rest of the flock to bits—
> they had lost the will to live.

Fine Rhetoric

A description of a gos:

> On the march, the rear guard of night's army
> was dyed red by the dawn, morning's
> effusive orator; night, his fine rhetoric
> now silenced, set in the west and I crossed
> the edges of darkness with a goshawk
> of great stamina, bloodthirsty,
> clad in an ample patterned mail coat;
> her brutal beak can smash brains to bits,
> and her mighty wings fill both my hands.

A Tender Lover

A description of a dog:

The dawn had not yet risen,
and the Pleiades swam in the trough
of gloom. Wrapped in a cloak of night,
I crossed the dark with a fleet, lean-
waisted saluki, his legs fraught
with speed, his nails like awls.
The gazelles were defenseless.
Death brought them an early dose
of poison—our saluki, a tender lover
with a deadly embrace.
Only blood would slake his thirst.
His sudden attack caught them off guard,
tearing them apart from head to hoof,
casting them aside like broken shells.

The Wind's Soft Hands

A description of a saker and dogs:

It was a day of pure bliss stolen
from Time, who paid us no heed
as we crossed the dark before sunrise
on haughty, long-necked horses,
through meadows awake with flowers
drenched in tears of rain—
as fragrant as musk pouches,
opened by the wind's soft hands,
scattered across the leas.
It was time for the quarry to die—
lean salukis, drop-eared hunters
like unfletched arrows—
were it not for their collars you'd think
a puff of wind might whisk them away.
Ground forces combined with aerial might—
working with sakers in yarak that tower,
then stoop from the sky, like buckets
dropped down a well by hasty hands
thirsty for water, our dogs snatched souls.
The hares' eardrums were burst by thwacks
like the cracks of date-palm spathes
split open by croppers.
Demon dogs with jaws of doom came early
to Qurayyah's jacks—running fast as the wind,

devouring the miles, rousing the wakeful quarry
all day.
    A graceful gazelle of a boy
passed a Bābil wine around, his waist swaying
with the weight of his plump buttocks.
You'd never recover from one of his looks.
His guardian paid no heed, as the boy's glance
glowed like a coal and my heart grew faint.

In Night's Tatters

A description of a gos:

> Like clear water in a muddy pond,
> dawn burst into bloom. The stars,
> like ailing eyes, were herded
> by the Pleiades shining like pearls
> among duller beads. Gemini lay
> on the horizon like a crown of leaves
> or buds on a branch. In the east,
> day, bright as a mouth of even teeth,
> shone like a lid on the earth.
> Wrapped in night's tatters,
> I traveled with a gos whose eyes
> scanned the horizon. Dyed each day
> with clots of blood, her hooked beak
> pierces and slices flesh; she binds to,
> and bones are split at the joints;
> her eyes never fail, burning like narcissi
> without petals; she sinks her talons,
> like half rings, and rips guts open;
> when quarry's sighted she's blessed
> with food, for her flights at prey never fail;
> she explodes when cast from the hand;
> unleashed, she's quicker than the fear
> in the eye of her prey—they see Death
> before they can scatter.

In the tall plants
of the fields, she spied swimmers on a lake,
like splashes of red in a twilight sky.
The wind blew the foam, as smiths whet
a blade's edge to make it easier to draw
from the sheath. Unswerving, she sped
like a fletched arrow and shredded
her targets. Her victims died on the spot;
the rest fainted at her swoop—
tufts of feathers on the ground.

Fluent in Human Speech

A description of a saker:

A night black as a raven's wing—
I'm out with a noble troop,
bringing doom to the quarry still asleep,
accompanied by a saker in yarak
with a stony crown and bulky wrist,
fluent in human speech. A brilliant expert—
footing sprung *ẓaby*s is her specialty,
her talons curved like round *nūn*s—
what fine calligraphy! Her mail shone
brightly in her patterned cloak,
like marks made by a stylus on parchment
or traces of kohl on an eyelid.
Then dawn burst and slashed the gloom,
a streak of white through black hair.

Doomed Fowl

A description of the pellet bow:

> We paid an early visit to a pond
> before it was draped in sunlight,
> the necks of the doomed fowl
> as if clad in jewels—
> all day long our bows fired eyeballs
> from their sockets at the birds.

Deft Hunters

A description of dogs:

> Pedigreed, of noble descent,
> deft hunters, lambent eyes—
> in their collars, they seem to grin
> with their long, thin pincer bites.

A Puff of Wind

A description of a saker:

A saker in yarak, with a stony crown
and bulky wrist, adept at speech,
a brilliant hunter with her curved talons
like a calligrapher's *nūn*s, her mail
brightly clad in a patterned cloak
like loops of *lām*s on parchment
or kohl penciled on eyelids.
A side-glance from her sharp eye
spotted ten geese in a duckweed pond.
She raked away on a true course,
a puff of wind, creeping like a thief.
With a wing flick she was on them,
ripping the guts from a nimble bird
in a thunderbolt display—
many perished, others fled away.

The troop rolled up their sleeves,
some hasty with their food,
others cooking it just right.
One of us, an admirer's devotion—
a lover beyond the pale of love—
drank wine, sheet-lightning bright.
Then dawn sliced through the gloom,
a streak of white through a dark head.
Praise God, the Generous Provider!

Her Thirsty Beak

A description of a peregrine, a crow, and waterfowl:

> It was a grim day for the wader
> beside the wind-rippled lake.
> Glistening fish squirmed in its beak,
> an assassin's evil dagger.
> Snatchfoot the peregrine came,
> rancorous, her thirsty beak
> out for blood. She sighted the wader.
> She laid a sudden trap: she avoided it,
> then ringed up, waited on, stooped—
> an avalanche, a thwack, a mess.

Like Torrents

A description of dogs:

> I sing of Flow, Drip, and Drop,
> sharp, slender dogs, tongues
> like branches in their mouths.
> Their lank hips, viewed from behind,
> quiver like lances, restlessly tugging
> on their chains. You watch them,
> in their leanness, climb the sand
> dunes like fingers outstretched,
> then rush on like torrents,
> pursuing the quarry
> with their pickax jaws.

Held Low in an Ambush

A description of the pellet bow:

> Held low in an ambush—
> God having decreed
> it shall inflict death today—
> it looks like a wet cloak
> fallen from a rope.
> May the archer who needs
> its pellets to secure food
> enjoy success!

Expert at Physiognomy

A description of a tiercel:

> Daybreak drove the murk away,
> dreams were divorced like wives,
> eyelids knitted, too small for sleep—
> I acted and roused noble comrades
> in a hurry to bridle their horses,
> and fetched my bold, battle-hardened tiercel,
> a paragon of beauty, able to feed
> a large army. On my retainer's hand,
> he sat like dawn clad in a mail coat
> of gloom, his mail like stippled marble
> or lines of writing traced by a fine stylus,
> letters and dots barely visible.
> He sees what lies concealed in hills
> and uplands with an eye that burns
> like a bonfire, deleting vast distances
> with his keen sight. Expert at physiognomy,
> he's a wiser hunter than we men;
> the scorpion sting of his bloody beak
> resembles a thumb making the sign for fifty.[2]
> He plucks out hidden bones, as you'd bend
> to pick up beads from a snapped necklace.
> His wings, striped like a *burd* lifted
> from a camel's hump, are spread wide
> for flight, and destroy all quarry they meet,
> quicker than a flash of lightning in a rain cloud,

the tail feathers like the edges of sharp blades.
Guided by his handler's left hand, he proceeds
to hunt his victims—pigeons and geese.

Sharp Knives

I have neither time nor tears for ruins
in Wahbīn or for faint traces in Karkh,
Qufṣ, Quṭrubbul, Ṭīzanābādh, or Kirkīn—
not even for a fawn whose love tortured me,
his curls like *nūn*s, daubed in scent.
Away from prying eyes, I gazed
at his face, thinking night had fallen
and I was lifting jewels and pearls
from a casket, or unfurling a *ṭirāzī* gown,
or unlocking flower gardens in full bloom.
Time startled my heart, forcing it to drink
life's bitterness, all aflutter like a bird
suddenly caught in a cage.
                                        Hurry!
Heal me with a wine chilled by the north wind,
for I'm overcome with grief—to think
that Nabataean farmers claimed
Khusro as their father! Who can take
a message to Khusro and Shīrīn?
They would have punished kings
for this claim, bellowing so loud
they'd scare farts from Hell's devils!

I crossed the dark, as dawn hurried the night
impaled on the sun's horn, accompanied
by goshawks following the course mapped
by their eyes between heaven and earth,

birds dressed for action, the plumage
above their arms like a sailor's breeches,
grabbing high-soaring birds in the air
(as the militia grasp men by their beards),
with four fingers on each foot, sharp knives
fashioned by God. Any quarry they see
is counted a catch when flying from the fist,
and, confident of killing any prey at whim,
they greedily shake their heads, like old men
who've seen how easily fortune can change.

The Drowsy Pleiades Set

A description of a bitch:

> A bitch taken on an early hunt
> by a troop of comrades released
> from Time's grip, with no thought
> for the future. On her return,
> the hunting ground emptied,
> she was like a white serpent
> at full stretch, or a spear fitted
> with her muzzle for its head.
> Some *ẓaby*s entered her field
> of vision, with a lean, watchful buck
> in the lead. The drowsy Pleiades set,
> but morning had lost its way,
> as if still lying undressed in bed.
> For this dog, whatever she spotted
> was fair prey.

Blood's Taste

A description of cheetahs:

> I sing of them speeding across the plain,
> hopping and skipping after their prey,
> relishing blood's taste—
> what life can survive such power?

Training or Instinct?

A description of dogs:

We crossed the feeble gloom as dawn revealed
our faces bringing to the oryx and *ẓaby*s of Dujayl
a pack of dogs as scrawny as convalescents.
On an early foray, they catch any prey the hunter wants,
never stopping until he gives the order.
When they're sicced, you won't see them miss the quarry,
held fast in their mouths without bloodshed—
training or instinct?—gingerly treading the ground
as if handling coals, called back by the hunter's shouts.

His Pickax Beak

A description of a tiercel and waterfowl:

A denizen of a distant river,
clear, burbling over pebbles,
with banks of rich well-trodden soil
and smiling spring flowers,
blossoms like peerless jewels
among fresh saplings—from dawn
to dusk, he sipped the dew's
saliva mixed with cold rainwater,
free of cares, deeming it his right
to eat and drink his fill,
protected from man by the jinn,
given dominion over the fish
he reaps with his pickax beak
like the tooth of an iron comb,
as if plucking arrows from a target.

I raided the bird with my tiercel,
life and death on a hunter's left hand,
his mail decorated in patterns;
his eyes, like a money changer's dinars,
pick out hidden shapes in the distance;
he's dressed in Qūhī breeches above arms
like burnished gold ingots; a proud warrior
in full armor, squinting with battle rage—
never likely to yield to insult or injury.

Notes

1 An echo of Q Fajr 89:12.

2 A reference to dactylonomy, or finger counting: see Pellat, "Ḥisāb al-ʿAḳd."

Glossary

ʿarfaj *Rhanterium epapposum*, a shrub grazed by livestock that grows in soft soil and is highly combustible when dried.

arms the legs of a raptor, from the thigh to the foot.

Bābil the Arabic name for Babylon, generally associated with wine production.

bind to a raptor "binds to" when she catches and holds her quarry in the air.

blaze (Ar. ghurrah) the white star-shaped mark on the forehead of a horse.

burd a mantle of striped woolen cloth manufactured in the Yemen.

cheetah (Ar. fahd) *Acinonyx jubatus*, trained for the hunt and carried on horseback behind the rider to preserve its strength.

covert undergrowth or a thicket in which game can hide.

crow (Ar. ghurāb) the hooded crow (*Corvus cornix*) or the South Eurasian raven (*Corvus corvus subcorax*); incorrectly identified by the copyist of MS Laleli 1728 as the quarry of the peregrine in Poems 42 and 51.

crown the head of a raptor.

Dujayl a river north of Baghdad.

farsakh a measure of distance, usually around 3.7 miles (just short of six kilometers).

fly at bolt a hawk "flies at bolt" when she flies at quarry straight from the fist.

fly from the fist the same as *fly at bolt*.

foot a raptor "foots" her prey when she grabs it with her feet and talons.

gazelle (Ar. ẓaby) the general term in Arabic for a gazelle, be it an *idmi*, *Gazella gazella*, the mountain gazelle, a species that lives on mountain ridges and desert plateaus, or a *rhim*, *Gazella arabica*, an Arabian subspecies of the mountain gazelle.

goshawk (Ar. bāz) *Accipiter gentilis*, the northern goshawk, a large and aggressive raptor; the female of the genus is noticeably larger than the male. When hunting, the goshawk will either hug the ground in flight or attack from a high soar. See also *tiercel*.

goose (Ar. iwazz) either *Anser albifrons*, the greater white-fronted goose; *Anser erythropus*, the lesser white-fronted goose; *Anser anser*, the greylag goose; or *Branta ruficolis*, the red-breasted goose.

ibis (Ar. bughth) *Geronticus eremita*, the northern bald ibis, the prey of the peregrine in Poems 42 and 51, mistakenly identified by the copyist of MS Laleli 1728 as the crow.

jilbab (Ar. jilbāb) a long and loose-fitting outer garment worn by women.

Karkh the west side of Baghdad below the Round City constructed by Caliph al-Manṣūr (r. 136–38/754–75).

khaṭṭī epithet of a spear shaft, imported from India to a place called al-Khaṭṭ, either in Yamāmah in the Arabian Peninsula or al-Baḥrayn.

Khusro the name of two Sassanid rulers, used in Arabic (*kisrā*) as a title, here Khusro II Parvīz (r. AD 590–628).

Kirkīn a suburb of Baghdad.

lām the Arabic letter *l* (ل).

maddah an orthographic sign written as a slightly curved line above the letter *alif* (آ).

mail the breast of a raptor.

mantle a raptor "mantles" when she spreads her wings and hunches over her prey.

Nabataean an Abbasid designation for the agriculturalists of the *sawād* of Iraq, the cultivated regions of lower Mesopotamia and the marshes between Kufa and Basra. According to the historian al-Ṭabarī, the Nabataeans of the *sawād* of Iraq were the Aramaeans who historically reigned in Babylonia and as far as the region of Mawṣil.

nawraj (or *nayraj*, *nawzaj*, or *nayzaj*) a domestically bred scent hound, probably a cross between a Kurdish sheepdog and a saluki.

net (Ar. shabak) a trap made of fine netting for catching birds, set up between two poles or trees.

niqab a head covering worn by women that conceals the face, with an aperture for the eyes.

nūn the Arabic letter *n* (ن).

onager (Ar. ḥimār waḥshī) *Equus hemionus hemippus*, the Syrian or Mesopotamian wild ass, an extinct subspecies that was native to Arabia. The onager, typically 660 pounds (300 kg) in weight and six and a half feet (two meters) in length, could reach speeds of thirty-seven miles (sixty km) per hour.

oryx (Ar. baqar waḥshī) *Oryx leucoryx*, the Arabian oryx, a subspecies of antelope distinctive for its straight horns and white hide, black facial and caudal stripes, and dark-brown legs. Oryx are perfectly adapted to desert conditions and can go for long periods without water.

pellet bow (Ar. qaws al-bunduq) a handheld bullet-shooting crossbow (also called a prodd or stone bow) constructed from wood, used for firing a pellet made of hardened clay, known in Arabic as *bunduq*, "hazelnut." The pellets were carried in pouches. Hunting with the pellet bow was a team sport.

peregrine (Ar. shahīn) *Falco peregrinus brookei*, the peregrine falcon, a powerful raptor, agile in the air, with a distinctive stoop on prey at great speeds, often catching its prey in the air. Peregrines have dark mustache marks under each eye.

pigeon (Ar. ḥamām) either *Columba livia palaestinae*, the Arabian rock dove, or *Columba livia gaddi*, the Iranian rock dove.

Qufṣ a people living in Kirmān-Baluchistan in southeastern Persia.

Qūhī adjective denoting an origin from Qūhistān, a mountainous and only partially arable province of Iran, renowned in the third/ninth century for the manufacture of fine linen textiles.

Qurayyah name of two areas in Baghdad.

Quṭrubbul a village in the vicinity of Baghdad renowned for the quality of its wines.

rake away a raptor, usually a falcon, "rakes away" when she flies too far while waiting on; see *wait on*.

ring up a raptor "rings up" when she climbs in a spiral.

saker (Ar. ṣaqr) *Falco cherrug milvipes*, the eastern saker falcon, a large rufous-brown falcon that prefers to hunt from a vantage point or from a height and surprise its prey. It has excellent stamina and will tail-chase its prey until the prey is exhausted. Females are larger than males.

saluki (Ar. salūqī) a sight hound widely used to hunt game, distinguished by its stamina and speed over long distances.

scent hound see *nawraj*.

scorpion either the fat-tailed scorpion (*Androctonus crassicauda*) or the lesser Asian scorpion (*Mesobuthus eupeus*). The former has a dark brown to black coloration, the latter yellow to light brown.

Shīrīn Christian wife and favorite of the Sassanian ruler Khusro II Parvīz (r. 590–628).

snake *Macrovipera lebetina*, the Lebetine (or blunt-nosed) viper found in Syria and Iraq.

sparrow hawk (Ar. bāshiq) *Accipiter nisus*, the Eurasian sparrow hawk, a small hawk known to hunt by employing an undulating flight to allow it to close in on its quarry before it can escape.

stoop a falcon "stoops" when she dives at quarry from a great height.

tiercel (Ar. zurraq) *Accipiter gentilis*, the male northern goshawk, noticeably smaller than the female, known in Arabic as *bāẓ*. See also *goshawk*.

ṭirāzī adjective from *ṭirāz*, a type of embroidery, usually in the form of a band, inscribed with the name of the ruler or patron, and sewn onto a ceremonial robe of honor.

Ṭīzanābādh a settlement between Kufa and al-Qādisiyyah much frequented by pleasure-seekers, renowned for its wines and taverns.

trap net (Ar. fakhkh) a trap for catching birds and gazelles, with a trip hazard placed under a suspended net.

Wahbīn either a sand dune or a mountain located in the great Dahnā' erg (sand sea) in the southeast of the Arabian Peninsula.

wait on a raptor "waits on" when she circles in the air at a height, until the game is sighted.

waterfowl (Ar. ṭayr al-mā') *Anas platyrhynchos*, the mallard or wild duck.

wrist the joint where a raptor's wings attach to her body.

yarak when a falcon or a hawk is described as "in yarak," it is in a fit and proper condition for flying—that is, hunting.

ẓaby see *gazelle*.

Bibliography

Barthes, Roland. *A Lover's Discourse*. Translated by Richard Howard. New York: Hill and Wang, 1978.

Bates, Catherine. *Masculinity and the Hunt: Wyatt to Spenser*. Oxford: Oxford University Press, 2016.

Bray, Julia. "Ibn al-Muʿtazz and Politics: The Question of the *Fuṣūl Qiṣār*." *Oriens* 38 (2010): 107–43.

Heinrichs, Wolfhart P. "Ibn al-Muʿtazz (1 November 861–17 December 908)." In *Arabic Literary Culture, 500–925*, edited by Michael Cooperson and Shawkat M. Toorawa, 164–71. Detroit: Thomson Gale, 2005.

Ibn Abī ʿAun [= ʿAwn]. *The Kitāb al-Tashbīhāt of Ibn Abī ʿAun*. Edited by M. ʿAbdul Muʿīd Khān. London: Luzac, 1950.

Ibn al-Muʿtazz. *Der Diwan des ʿAbdallāh ibn al-Muʿtazz*. Edited by Bernhard Lewin. 2 vols. Istanbul: Staatsdruckerei, 1945 and 1950.

———. *Fuṣūl al-tamāthīl fī tabāshīr al-surūr*. Edited by Makkī Sayyid al-Jasīm and Muḥammad Makkī al-Jasīm. Baghdad: Dār al-Shuʾūn al-Thaqāfiyyah al-ʿĀmmah, 1989.

———. *Kitāb al-Badīʿ of ʿAbd Allāh Ibn al-Muʿtazz*. Edited by Ignatius Kratchkovsky. London: Luzac, 1935.

———. *Min Fuṣūl Ibn al-Muʿtazz wa-rasāʾilihi wa-nuṣūṣ min kutubihi al-mafqūdah wa-akhbārihi*. Edited by Yūnus Aḥmad al-Sāmarrāʾī. Baghdad: Wizārat al-Thaqāfah, Dār al-Shuʾūn al-Thaqāfiyyah al-ʿĀmmah, 2002.

———. *Ṭabaqāt al-shuʿarāʾ al-muḥdathīn fī madḥ al-khulafāʾ wa-l-wuzarāʾ*. Edited by ʿAbd al-Sattār Aḥmad Farrāj. Cairo: Dār al-Maʿārif, 1968.

Kratchkovsky, Ignatius. "Le *Kitāb al-Ādāb* d'Ibn al-Muʿtazz." *Le Monde Oriental* 18 (1924): 56–121.

Montgomery, James E., ed. and trans. *Fate the Hunter: Early Arabic Hunting Poems*. New York: New York University Press, 2023.

Pellat, Ch. "Ḥisāb al-ʿAḳd." *Encyclopaedia of Islam, Second Edition*. Brill Online, 2012.

Al-Shabushtī. *The Book of Monasteries*. Edited and translated by Hilary Kilpatrick. New York: New York University Press, 2023.

Stoetzer, W. "Sarīʿ." *Encyclopaedia of Islam, Second Edition*. Brill Online, 2012.

Al-Ṣūlī. *Ashʿār awlād al-khulafāʾ min Kitāb al-Awrāq*. Edited by J. Heyworth-Dunne. London: Luzac, 1935.

Turberville, George. *Epitaphes, Epigrams, Songs and Sonets*. London: Henry Denham, 1567.

Further Reading

Ali, Samer M. *Arabic Literary Salons in the Islamic Middle Ages: Poetry, Public Performance, and the Presentation of the Past.* Notre Dame, IN: University of Notre Dame Press, 2010.

Arazi, Albert. "Poétique et politique dans *Kitāb al-ṭabaqāt* d'Ibn al-Muʿtazz." *Jerusalem Studies in Arabic and Islam* 30 (2005): 264–92.

Bates, Catherine. *Masculinity, Gender and Identity in the English Renaissance Lyric.* Cambridge: Cambridge University Press, 2007.

Bauer, Thomas. *A Culture of Ambiguity: An Alternative History of Islam.* Translated by Hinrich Biesterfeldt and Tricia Tunstall. New York: Columbia University Press, 2021.

Bonebakker, S. A. "Ibn al-Muʿtazz and *Kitāb al-Badīʿ*." In *ʿAbbasid Belles-Lettres*, edited by Julia Ashtiany et al., 388–411. Cambridge: Cambridge University Press, 1990.

Calasso, Roberto. *The Celestial Hunter.* Translated by Richard Dixon. London: Penguin, 2020.

Fahd, Toufic. "Nabaṭ." *Encyclopaedia of Islam, Second Edition.* Brill Online, 2012.

Ibn al-Muʿtazz. *Dīwān ashʿār al-Amīr Abī l-ʿAbbās ʿAbd Allāh ibn Muḥammad al-Muʿtazz bi-llāh al-khalīfah al-ʿAbbāsī.* Edited by Muḥammad Badīʿ Sharīf. Cairo: Dār al-Maʿārif, 1977–78.

———. *Dīwān shiʿr Ibn al-Muʿtazz.* Edited by Yūnus al-Sāmarrāʾī. 3 vols. Beirut: ʿĀlam al-Kutub li-l-Ṭibāʿah wa-l-Nashr wa-l-Tawzīʿ, 1997.

Lang, C. "Muʿtaḍid als Prinz und Regent, ein historisches Heldengedicht von Ibn el Muʿtazz." *Zeitschrift der Deutschen Morgenländischen*

Gesellschaft 40 (1886): 563–611; *Zeitschrift der Deutschen Morgenländischen Gesellschaft* 41 (1887): 232–79.

Lewin, B. "Ibn al-Muʿtazz." *Encyclopaedia of Islam, Second Edition.* Brill Online, 2012.

Massignon, Louis. *The Passion of al-Hallaj, Mystic and Martyr of Islam.* Translated by Herbert Mason. 4 vols. Princeton, NJ: Princeton University Press, 2019.

Mattock, John N. "A Political Poem of Ibn al-Muʿtazz." *Occasional Papers of the School of Abbasid Studies* 4 (1992): 51–61.

Montgomery, James E. "Review of Jocelyn Sharlet, *Patronage and Poetry in the Islamic World.*" *Der Islam* 92, no. 1 (2015): 287–91.

Osti, Letizia. *History and Memory in the Abbasid Caliphate: Writing the Past in Medieval Arabic Literature.* London: I. B. Tauris, 2022.

Ouyang, Wen-chin. *Literary Criticism in Medieval Arabic-Islamic Culture: The Making of a Tradition.* Edinburgh: Edinburgh University Press, 1997.

Rosenmayer, Thomas G. *The Green Cabinet: Theocritus and the European Pastoral Lyric.* Berkeley, CA: University of California Press, 1973.

Schoeler, Gregor. *Arabische Naturduchtung.* Beirut: Franz Steiner Verlag, 1974.

Sedgwick, Eve Kosofsky. *Between Men: English Literature and Male Homosocial Desire.* New York: Columbia University Press, 2016.

Sharlet, J. *Patronage and Poetry in the Islamic World: Social Mobility and Status in the Medieval Middle East and Central Asia.* London: I. B. Tauris, 2011.

Spearing, A. C. *The Medieval Poet as Voyeur.* Cambridge: Cambridge University Press, 1993.

Stetkevych, Jaroslav. *The Hunt in Arabic Poetry: From Heroic to Lyric to Metapoetic.* Notre Dame, IN: University of Notre Dame Press, 2016.

Sourdel, Dominique. *Le vizirat ʿabbāside de 749 à 936 (132 à 324 de l'Hégire).* Damascus: Institut Français de Damas, 1959–60.

Index

birds (cont.)
slaughtering of, 24; song birds, xviii; waterfowl, xviii, 63, 73; wind described as, 46–7. *See also* birds of prey; wings
birds of prey: binding to, 52; crowns, 24, 37, 59, 62; footing, 59; mail, xx, xxi, 25, 26, 34, 37, 53, 59, 62, 66, 73; mantling, xix, 42; raking away, 62; ringing up, 63; sakers, xxi, xxxii, 13, 15, 42, 51, 55, 59, 62; stooping, xix; swooping, xx, 58; talons, xix, xxi, 9, 24, 27, 34, 35, 51, 57, 59, 62; wrists, 23, 42, 49, 59, 62; in yarak, xix, xxi, xxii, 13, 15, 55, 59, 62. *See also* beaks; falconry; flying; goshawks; tiercels; wings
bismillah, 38
blades, 11, 37, 58, 67
blaze (*ghurrah*), 8, 23, 36, 46
blocks, xx, 11, 19
blood: beaks dyed by, 12, 57, 66; blood oaths, 9; bloodthirst, xxv, 44, 53, 54, 63; dogs drinking, 4; drenching talons, 27; exchanging flesh for, 6; no bloodshed, 11, 17, 18, 20, 28, 72; relishing taste of, 44, 71; shedding of, 8, 14, 34, 51
bones, 37, 57, 66
bonfires, 66
Book of Monasteries (al-Shabushtī), xviii
books, 9
boots, ix, 52
Borges, Jorge Luis, xxxviii
boulders, 23, 37
bowls, 39
bows, xxviii, 31, 33, 40–1, 60, 65
boys, xxi, xxxii, 56
bracelets, 23
brains, 53
breasts, ix, 20, 40
breeches, 12, 69, 73
breezes, 4, 30
Brief Statements (Ibn al-Muʿtazz), xxvii
brows, 8, 24
buck, 70
buckets, xix, 15, 55
burd (mantle), 66
buttocks, 36, 56

cages, 68
calligraphy, xx–xxi, 59, 62
calls, 3–4, 9, 21, 72
camels, 3, 23, 24, 66
campsites, xxviii
canals, xxxv, 12
caskets, 68
cheeks, xx, 16
cheetahs (*fahd*), xx, xxxi, 16, 33, 43, 71
chests, 9, 16, 20
children, 47. *See also* babies; youth
Christians, xx, xxviii, 34
clay, 40
cloaks, xxi, 3, 23, 30, 36, 54, 59, 62, 65
cloisters, 28
clouds, 7, 13, 23, 30, 39, 42, 50, 52, 66
coals, 16, 56, 72
coats, xx, 3, 10, 25, 31, 37, 53, 66
cobblers, 3
coins, 47
collars, 26, 34, 38, 55, 61
combs, 50, 73
communal feasts of meat sharing, xviii, xxi, xxii, xxviii, xxxi, xxxii, xxxvii, 16, 24, 47, 49
comrades, xxii, xxx, 12, 18, 29, 45, 66, 70

convalescents, 72
cotton, 12, 24
courtly society, xxiv, xxvi–xxviii, xxxi
coverts, 45
cows, 22
creeks, 34
croppers, 55
crows (*ghurāb*), 11, 17, 52, 63
crystal, 39
cups, 36
curls, 68
cypress, 13

daggers, 28, 37, 63
darkness: of night, xviii, xxii, 3, 7, 36, 62; crossing of, 8, 9, 13, 17, 26, 30, 31, 36, 38, 40, 43, 44, 49, 53, 54, 55, 68; goshawks in, 25, 53; horses reaching water in, xix, 32
date palms, 13, 37, 46, 55
dates, 13
dawn: and darkness, 6, 25, 26, 38, 40, 44, 66; described as blaze, 23, 36; described as clear water, 57; described as gray/white hair, 13, 59, 62; described as morning's orator, 53; and dew, 4, 73; dressing/undressing by, xx, 3, 11, 17, 18, 34; to dusk, 22, 73; and light, 29, 30, 38; pre-dawn, xvii, xviii, xix, xx, xxi, xxx, 25, 29, 34, 38, 40, 54, 68; revealing of faces, 72; and salukis' hunger, 22; showing of teeth, 9; and stars, 6, 23, 54, 57; tiercel sitting as, 66. *See also* dusk; morning; night
day, xx, 9, 16, 24, 34, 39, 43, 55–6, 57, 60, 63, 66
daybreak, 45, 66
death: and birth, 7; cheating of, 47; by cheetah, 16; of clouds, 7; death knells, 26; of dogs, 31; by dogs, 3, 38, 50, 54, 55; fear of, ix, 57; by goshawk, 57–8; meeting Death, 9, 12, 20, 52; by pellet bows, 65; ritual of, xxii; saliva of, 20; sparrow hawks' love of, 21; by swords, 35; by tiercels, 73
debauchery, xxxiii, 36
degeneracy, xxvii
demons, 30, 55
desert, xviii, xxviii, 10, 17, 18, 20, 33, 46, 50
destiny, 47
devils, 38, 68
dew, 4, 6, 45, 73
al-Dimashqī, Abū l-Ḥasan Aḥmad ibn Ṣaʿīd, xxiv
dinars, 34, 45, 73
dirhams, 36
divining arrows, 43
dogs: bitches, xx, 3, 11, 17, 18, 19, 31, 70; bloodthirst, 44, 54; coat, 3, 10; death of, 31; descent, 61; described as demons, 30, 55; dogfights, 44; ears, 3, 30, 50, 55; eyes, 3, 10, 11, 17, 18, 61; hips, 22, 38, 48, 54, 64; and hunters, xxii, xxxi, 3–4, 17, 48, 70; kennel-bred, 44; leashes, 30, 31, 38, 50, 64; legs, 30, 54; no shedding of blood by, 11, 17, 28, 72; in poems' text, 3–4, 10, 17, 28, 30, 38–9, 44, 45, 48, 50, 54, 55–6, 61, 64, 70, 72; salukis, xxviii, xxxii, 11, 22, 28, 50, 54, 55–6 ; scent hounds, 44, 45; speed, xviii, xxi, 3–4, 17, 28, 30, 31, 38–9, 45, 54, 55–6, 64, 70; teeth, 11, 17, 18, 61

dots, xx, 45, 66
dreams, xx, 66
duckweed, 62
Dujayl, 72
dusk, 4, 22, 73. *See also* dawn
dust, 3, 8, 23, 24, 30, 37, 42, 43, 50

earrings, 50
ears, 3, 13, 30, 50, 55
embroidery, 36, 45
emirs, 12
eyes: of birds, 40, 52; blink of an eye, 3, 13; of cheetahs, xx, 16, 43; of clouds, 7; color of, when inflamed, xix, 32; color of dinars, 34; described as gold nails, 12; of dogs, 3, 10, 11, 17, 18, 61; eyeballs, 60; eyebrows, xix, 24; eyelids, xix, xx, xxi, 24, 32, 34, 59, 62, 66; field of vision, 70; glances, 13, 18, 56, 62; of goshawks, xx, 12, 24, 26, 37, 57, 68; houri-eyed girls, 38; looks, xxxii, 56; of love object, xxxii, xxxiii, 36, 56; of oryxes, 38; of prey, 40, 57; prying, 68; of sakers, 13, 15, 51, 62; of saplings, 36; seeing in darkness, 31; sight, 34, 43, 57, 63, 66; stars described as, 45, 57; tears, 7, 36, 40, 55, 68; of tiercels, 73, 66

fahd (cheetahs), xx, xxxi, 16, 33, 43, 71
falconers, 13, 67
falconry, xviii–xix, xxxvii
falcons: peregrine falcons, 52, 63; sakers, xxi, xxxii, 13, 15, 42, 51, 55, 59, 62
farsakh (measure of distance), 27
Fate, 38, 40, 47
fawns, 4, 68
fear, ix, xxxiii, 3, 9, 27, 37, 52, 57–8
feathers, xx, xxii, 12, 20, 24, 26, 58, 67
feet, ix, xix, 13, 23, 30, 63, 69
fetuses, 46
fields, xxi, xxxii, 4, 6, 58
fife, 34
fingers, 64, 69, 75n2
fire, xvii, xxii, 5, 13, 23, 24, 35, 41, 43, 60, 66
fish, xxi, xxii, 63, 73
flags, 23
flames, 13. *See also* fire
flanks, 3
flesh, 4, 6, 57
flocks, xviii, 41, 52
floods, 45
flowers, xxxii, 3, 4, 36, 55, 68, 73
flying: at bolt, 42; cheetahs, 16; crows, 52; like arrows, 21, 31; of goshawks, 57, 69; of pellets, 40; raking away, 62; ready to, xix, 49; ringing up, 63; sakers, 13–4, 15, 42, 55; stooping, xix, 14, 15, 55, 63; tiercels, 9, 49, 66; waiting on, 63
foal, 46
folly, 8
forays, 9, 72
forelocks, 46
fortune, xxix, 69
fowl, 60
fragrance, 55
fringes, xx, 3, 12, 34, 36, 40
fronds, 13

gazelles (*ẓabys*), xviii, xxxii–xxxiii, 3, 11, 16, 30, 36, 50, 54, 56, 59, 70, 72
geese (*iwazz*), 14, 15, 42, 62, 67
Gemini, 6, 23, 57

generals, 25, 27, 29
ghazal. See love
ghurāb (crows), 11, 17, 52, 63
ghurrah (blaze), 8, 23, 36, 46
girls, xxxii, 8, 23, 38
gloom, 23, 38, 54, 59, 62, 66, 72. *See also* darkness; dusk; night
gloves, xix, xxxiii, 13, 34, 37
goblets, xviii, 8, 13
God, xxiv, xxix, 13, 31, 47, 62, 65, 69
gold, xx, 10, 12, 16, 73
goshawks (*bāz*): about, xix, xx, xxix, xxxii–xxxiii; described as generals, 12, 25, 27, 29, 34; eyes, 12, 24, 26, 34, 37, 53, 68; and love, xxxii–xxxiii, 36–7; in poems' text, 9, 12, 24, 25, 27, 29, 34–5, 36–7, 45, 53, 57, 68; and rulership, xxviii, xxix, 34–5, 69; speed, 57; and tiercels, 9; wings, 24, 26, 37, 53. *See also* tiercels
gowns, xx, 16, 36, 46, 68
grapes, 8
Greek philosophy and science, xxvi
guts, 57, 62

hair: gray, 8, 13, 44; of hags, 4; of horses, 23, 46; of night, 3, 11, 50, 59; white, 38, 59. *See also* blaze
ḥamām (pigeons), 67
Ḥanbalī movement, xxvi
hands, xix, 12, 21, 36, 53, 55, 57, 66, 67, 73
harems, 46
hares, xxxii, 17, 18, 44, 55
hauberks, 29
hawks: about, xvii, xix, xx, xxi, xxix, xxxii, xxxiii; hawking, xxxvii; sparrow hawks, 21; tiercels, xix, 9, 49, 66–7, 73. *See also* birds of prey; goshawks
heads, 8, 12, 17, 24, 54, 62, 69
hearts, xxxii, 8, 38, 40, 56, 68
Hell, 68
herds, xviii, 4, 6, 11, 57
heroic masculinity, xxx–xxxi
hides, 31
hijabs, 17, 18
hills, 42, 66
ḥimār waḥshī (onager jacks), xviii, xxix, xxx, xxxi, 46
hips, 22, 38, 64
homosocial desire, xxxi–xxxii, 36–7, 55–6
hoppers, 26
horizons, xix, 3, 17, 23, 32, 57
horns, 68
horsemen, 30
horses: blazes, 8, 23, 36, 46; carrying cheetahs, 43; feet, 23; galloping, 38, 45; hooves, xviii, xix, 8, 13, 23, 26, 30, 39; moving like a river in spate, 8, 13; necks, 55; pasterns, 23; in poems' text, 8, 13, 23–4, 26, 30, 32, 36, 38, 43, 45, 46, 55, 66; ribs, 23; saddles, 45; spines, 23; withers, 23
hounds, xvii, xviii, xxi, xxviii, 44, 45, 48. *See also* dogs, salukis
houndsmen, 28
hubris, 41
humps, 66
hunters: becoming victims, xxxii; death described as, 52; dog handlers, 48, 72; and dogs, 48, 55, 61, 72; hungry and poor, 48; incompetent, 5; sakers, 62; tiercels, xix, 9, 49, 66–7, 73

nūn (Arabic letter), xxi, 59, 62, 68
nurses, 47

oaths, xxiv, 9
onager jacks (*ḥimār waḥshī*), xviii, xxix, xxx, xxxi, 46
orators, 53
oryxes (*baqar waḥshī*), 3, 22, 23, 38, 45, 72

pages, xxi, 27
palm leaves, 13, 46
palms. *See* date palms
Paragon of Eloquence (al-Sharīf al-Raḍī), xxvii
parchment, xxi, 34, 37, 59, 62
pasterns, 23
paws, 28
pearls, 22, 50, 57, 68. *See also* jewels
pellet bows (*qaws al-bunduq*), xxviii, 40–1, 60, 65
pellets, xxviii, 5, 40–1, 60, 65
pens, 3
peregrine falcons (*shahīn*), 52, 63
Persian, 27, 34
petals, 3, 57
physiognomy, 66
pickaxes, 64, 73
pigeons (*ḥamām*), 67
pillions, xx, 16
pincers, 61
pitch, xx, 7, 34
plants, 58
plectrums, 34
Pleiades, xxv, 23, 43, 50, 54, 57, 70
plumage, 69
poetry: boasts, xxviii–xxix; by Ibn al-Muʿtazz, xvii–xxii, xxiii, xxv–xxxiii, xxxixn1; meter, xxviii–xxix; Modernist, xxv–xxvi, xxviii; motifs, xxviii–xxxiii; "novel" (*badīʿ*) style, xxvi; vaunts, xxviii–xxix
poison, 54
polo mallets, 23
ponds, 14, 15, 57, 60, 62
pouches, 40, 55
poverty, 48
prey. *See* quarry and prey
prison, xxiv, 20

Qabīḥah, xxiv
qaws al-bunduq (pellet bows), xxviii, 40–1, 60, 65
quarry and prey: and cheetahs, 16, 43, 71; and dogs, 3–4, 28, 38, 44, 45, 50, 54, 55–6, 64, 70, 72; and goshawks, xxviii, xxix, 12, 26, 34–5, 37, 45, 57–8, 69; and heroic masculinity, xxx–xxxi; and horses, 8, 46; and love, xxxi–xxxiii; onager as, xviii; and peregrines, 52; in poems' text, 3–4, 8, 12, 14, 16, 21, 26, 28, 34–5, 37, 38, 43, 44, 45, 46, 50, 52, 54, 55–6, 57–8, 59, 64, 66–7, 69, 70, 71, 72; sacred bond between hunter and, xxii, xxx; and sakers, 14, 55–6, 59; seeing Death, 16, 57; sniffing out of, 44, 45; and sparrow hawks, 21; terrifying of, xxxiii, 37; and tiercels, 66–7. *See also specific animals*; victims
Qufṣ, 68
Qūhī breeches, 73
Qur'an, xxv–xxvi, 36
Qurayyah, xxxv, 55
Quṭrubbul, 68

races, 30, 38, 46
rain: and clouds, 7, 52, 66; pellets compared to raining stones, xxii, 41; in poems' text, 3, 7, 36, 39, 45, 52, 55, 64, 66, 73; rainwater, 73; tears of, 7, 45, 55; torrents, 39, 64; washing leas, 36. *See also* clouds
rats, 20, 46
ravens, 59
rhetoric, xxv, xxvii, 53
ribs, 23
rivers, 8, 13, 40, 73
robes, 109
rocks, 15, 87, 105
ropes, 97, 147
ruins, 153
rulership, xxviii–xxx, 34–5, 69

saddles, 45
safflower, 37
saffron, 48
sailors, 69
saker falcons (*ṣaqr*), xxi, xxxii, 13, 15, 42, 51, 55, 59, 62
saliva, 20, 73
salukis (sight hounds), xxviii, xxxii, 11, 22, 28, 50, 54, 55–6
Samarra, xxiv–xxv
sand dunes, 64
saplings, 36, 73
sāqī (wine servers), xxi, xxxii–xxxiii, 36–7, 56
ṣaqr (saker falcons), xxi, xxxii, 13, 15, 42, 51, 55, 59, 62
Sassanian learning, xxvi–xxvii
scent, 36, 68
scent hounds (*nawraj*), 44, 45
scorpions, 3, 66
script, xxi, 27
serpents, 70
shabak (nets), xviii, 20
al-Shabushtī, xxviii
shadows, 52
shahīn (peregrine falcons), 52, 63
al-Sharīf al-Raḍī, xxvii
sheaths, 11, 12, 18, 28, 58. *See also* blades; knives
sheets, 30, 62
shells, 54
Shīrīn (wife of Khusro II Parvīz), 68
shoes, 48
shuʿūbiyyah controversy, xxvi
silver, 25, 47
skins, xx, 4, 9, 34
sky: dust clouds in, 30; illuminated by sun, 36; and light, 40; and pellets, xxii, 5, 41; sky dust, 3; and stars, 6, 50; stooping from, 55; tiercel taking to, 6, 49; twilight, 58
slaves, xx, 9
sleeves, xix, 37, 62
smallpox, xix, 39
smiling, 8, 36, 45, 73
smiths, 43, 58
snakes, xx, 4, 10, 17, 18
society, ills of, xxvii, 47
souls, 12, 16, 25, 47, 55
spadixes, 46
sparrow hawks (*bāshiq*), 21
spathes, 37, 55
spearheads, 12, 20
spears, 9, 12, 20, 23, 42, 70
spear shafts, 9
speech, xxvi, xxvii, 59, 62
speed: of cheetahs, 33, 71; of dogs, xviii, xxi, 3–4, 17, 28, 30, 31, 38–9, 45, 54, 55–6, 64, 70; of gazelles, 33; of goshawks, 57; of horses, xix,

speed (cont.)
xxxi, 13, 23, 46; of onagers, xxx–xxxi; quicker than a blink, 3, 6, 13; of sakers, 13, 59; of tiercels, 9, 66
spines, 23, 50
squadrons, 34
staffs, 46
stars: described as watery-eyed, 45; dogs described as, xviii, xx, 3, 11, 17, 19; Gemini, 6, 23, 57; and night, 3, 45; Pleiades, 23, 43, 50, 54, 57, 70; quenching the soil, 7; shooting stars, xviii, 3, 49; tiercel described as, 49
storms, xviii, xxviii, 8, 23, 30, 39, 45
strings, 40, 42
styluses, xxi, 6, 59, 66
sun, xxviii, 23, 27, 36, 49, 55, 60, 68
sunlight, 60
sunrise, 23, 55
Suspended Ode (*Muʿallaqah*) (Imru' al-Qays), xxviii
swords, 18, 35
syncretism, xxvi–xxvii

table companion (*nadīm*), xxvii
tails, 3, 13, 20, 37, 50, 67
ṭardiyyāt (hunting poems), xxviii–xxxiii, xxxvii
Ṭardiyyāt (Ibn al-Muʿtazz): about, xxviii; translation, xxxvii
targets, xxii, 30, 58, 73
ṭayr al-mā' (waterfowl), xviii, 63, 73
tears, 7, 36, 40, 55, 68
teeth: brightness of, 57; of combs, 50, 73; of dawn, 3, 9, 57; of dogs, 11, 17, 18, 61; of gazelles, 36; of saplings, 36; white teeth on red lips, 3
temples, 46
tents, 46
Thaʿlab, Aḥmad ibn Yaḥyā, xxiv
thieves, 62
throats, 46
thumbs, 66
thunder, 7, 30, 62
thunderbolts, 62
tiercels (*zurraq*), xix, 9, 49, 66–7, 73. *See also* goshawks
time, xxix, 12, 34, 38, 45, 52, 55, 68, 70
ṭirāzī (type of embroidery), 68
Ṭīzanābādh, 68
tongues, 28, 64
torrents, 39, 64
train feathers, 12
traps, xviii, 20, 63
trees, 13. *See also* date palms
Turkish, xix, xx, xxiv, 16
turquoise, 23
tweezers, 44
tyrants, 35

veils, 12
venom, xix, 13
victims, xxxii, 4, 35, 58, 67. *See also* quarry and prey

waders, 63
Wahbīn, 68
waists, 36, 54, 56
warriors, xvii, 20, 45, 73
water: birds in, 27, 34, 63, 73; dawn described as, 57; drinking of, 47, 55; horses in, xix, 23, 32; rainwater, 73; spilling from a jug, xix, 13; stars described as watery-eyed, 45; and thunder clouds, 7; water carriers, 5; and wells, xix, 14, 15, 55. *See also* lakes; ponds; rivers

water bugs, 46
waterfowl (*ṭayr al-māʾ*), xviii, 63, 73
al-Wāthiq bi-llāh, Hārūn (caliph), xxiv
weapons. *See* arrows; bows; knives; lances; spears; swords
wells, xix, 14, 15, 55
whips, 13, 16, 50
whirlwinds, 30, 46
wind, xix, 11, 23, 28, 46, 55–6, 58, 62, 63, 68
wine: courtly etiquette, xxiv; cups, 36; goshawk's mail compared to, xx, 26; in monasteries, xxviii; in poems' text, 26, 36, 45, 56, 62, 68; wine servers, xxi, xxxii–xxxiii, 36–7, 56
wings: of air, 3; broken, 41; of crows, 11; of goshawks, xix, xxxiii, 24, 26, 37, 53; of ravens, 59; of sakers, 42, 62; of tiercels, 49, 66; and wind, 46–7
withers, 23
wives, xx, 66
wombs, 46

Yemeni, 36
youth, xviii, 8, 9, 11, 38

ẓabys. *See* gazelles
zurraq (tiercels), xix, 9, 49, 66–7, 73. *See also* goshawks

About the NYU Abu Dhabi Research Institute

جامعة نيويورك ابوظبي
NYU ABU DHABI

The Library of Arabic Literature is a research center affiliated with NYU Abu Dhabi and is supported by a grant from the NYU Abu Dhabi Research Institute.

The NYU Abu Dhabi Research Institute is a world-class center of cutting-edge and innovative research, scholarship, and cultural activity. It supports centers that address questions of global significance and local relevance and allows leading faculty members from across the disciplines to carry out creative scholarship and high-level research on a range of complex issues with depth, scale, and longevity that otherwise would not be possible.

From genomics and climate science to the humanities and Arabic literature, Research Institute centers make significant contributions to scholarship, scientific understanding, and artistic creativity. Centers strengthen cross-disciplinary engagement and innovation among the faculty, build critical mass in infrastructure and research talent at NYU Abu Dhabi, and have helped make the university a magnet for outstanding faculty, scholars, students, and international collaborations.

About the Translator

James E. Montgomery is Sir Thomas Adams's Professor of Arabic, Fellow of Trinity Hall at the University of Cambridge, and an Executive Editor of the Library of Arabic Literature. In 2024 he was elected Fellow of the British Academy.

The Library of Arabic Literature

For more details on individual titles, visit www.libraryofarabicliterature.org

Classical Arabic Literature: A Library of Arabic Literature Anthology
Selected and translated by Geert Jan van Gelder (2012)

A Treasury of Virtues: Sayings, Sermons, and Teachings of ʿAlī, by al-Qāḍī al-Quḍāʿī, with the *One Hundred Proverbs* attributed to al-Jāḥiẓ
Edited and translated by Tahera Qutbuddin (2013)

The Epistle on Legal Theory, by al-Shāfiʿī
Edited and translated by Joseph E. Lowry (2013)

Leg over Leg, by Aḥmad Fāris al-Shidyāq
Edited and translated by Humphrey Davies (4 volumes; 2013–14)

Virtues of the Imām Aḥmad ibn Ḥanbal, by Ibn al-Jawzī
Edited and translated by Michael Cooperson (2 volumes; 2013–15)

The Epistle of Forgiveness, by Abū l-ʿAlāʾ al-Maʿarrī
Edited and translated by Geert Jan van Gelder and Gregor Schoeler (2 volumes; 2013–14)

The Principles of Sufism, by ʿĀʾishah al-Bāʿūniyyah
Edited and translated by Th. Emil Homerin (2014)

The Expeditions: An Early Biography of Muḥammad, by Maʿmar ibn Rāshid
Edited and translated by Sean W. Anthony (2014)

Two Arabic Travel Books
Accounts of China and India, by Abū Zayd al-Sīrāfī
Edited and translated by Tim Mackintosh-Smith (2014)
Mission to the Volga, by Aḥmad ibn Faḍlān
Edited and translated by James Montgomery (2014)

Disagreements of the Jurists: A Manual of Islamic Legal Theory, by al-Qāḍī al-Nuʿmān
Edited and translated by Devin J. Stewart (2015)

Consorts of the Caliphs: Women and the Court of Baghdad, by Ibn al-Sāʿī
Edited by Shawkat M. Toorawa and translated by the Editors of the Library of Arabic Literature (2015)

What ʿĪsā ibn Hishām Told Us, by Muḥammad al-Muwayliḥī
Edited and translated by Roger Allen (2 volumes; 2015)

The Life and Times of Abū Tammām, by Abū Bakr Muḥammad ibn Yaḥyā al-Ṣūlī
Edited and translated by Beatrice Gruendler (2015)

The Sword of Ambition: Bureaucratic Rivalry in Medieval Egypt, by ʿUthmān ibn Ibrāhīm al-Nābulusī
Edited and translated by Luke Yarbrough (2016)

Brains Confounded by the Ode of Abū Shādūf Expounded, by Yūsuf al-Shirbīnī
Edited and translated by Humphrey Davies (2 volumes; 2016)

Light in the Heavens: Sayings of the Prophet Muḥammad, by al-Qāḍī al-Quḍāʿī
Edited and translated by Tahera Qutbuddin (2016)

Risible Rhymes, by Muḥammad ibn Maḥfūẓ al-Sanhūrī
Edited and translated by Humphrey Davies (2016)

A Hundred and One Nights
Edited and translated by Bruce Fudge (2016)

The Excellence of the Arabs, by Ibn Qutaybah
Edited by James E. Montgomery and Peter Webb
Translated by Sarah Bowen Savant and Peter Webb (2017)

Scents and Flavors: A Syrian Cookbook
Edited and translated by Charles Perry (2017)

Arabian Satire: Poetry from 18th-Century Najd, by Ḥmēdān al-Shwēʿir
Edited and translated by Marcel Kurpershoek (2017)

In Darfur: An Account of the Sultanate and Its People, by Muḥammad ibn ʿUmar al-Tūnisī
Edited and translated by Humphrey Davies (2 volumes; 2018)

War Songs, by ʿAntarah ibn Shaddād
Edited by James E. Montgomery
Translated by James E. Montgomery with Richard Sieburth (2018)

Arabian Romantic: Poems on Bedouin Life and Love, by ʿAbdallah ibn Sbayyil
Edited and translated by Marcel Kurpershoek (2018)

Dīwān ʿAntarah ibn Shaddād: A Literary-Historical Study, by James E. Montgomery (2018)

Stories of Piety and Prayer: Deliverance Follows Adversity, by al-Muḥassin ibn ʿAlī al-Tanūkhī
Edited and translated by Julia Bray (2019)

Tajrīd sayf al-himmah li-stikhrāj mā fī dhimmat al-dhimmah: A Scholarly Edition of ʿUthmān ibn Ibrāhīm al-Nābulusī's Text, by Luke Yarbrough (2019)

The Philosopher Responds: An Intellectual Correspondence from the Tenth Century, by Abū Ḥayyān al-Tawḥīdī and Abū ʿAlī Miskawayh
Edited by Bilal Orfali and Maurice A. Pomerantz
Translated by Sophia Vasalou and James E. Montgomery (2 volumes; 2019)

The Discourses: Reflections on History, Sufism, Theology, and Literature—
Volume One, by al-Ḥasan al-Yūsī
Edited and translated by Justin Stearns (2020)

Impostures, by al-Ḥarīrī
Translated by Michael Cooperson (2020)

Maqāmāt Abī Zayd al-Sarūjī, by al-Ḥarīrī
Edited by Michael Cooperson (2020)

The Yoga Sutras of Patañjali, by Abū Rayḥān al-Bīrūnī
Edited and translated by Mario Kozah (2020)

The Book of Charlatans, by Jamāl al-Dīn ʿAbd al-Raḥīm al-Jawbarī
Edited by Manuela Dengler
Translated by Humphrey Davies (2020)

A Physician on the Nile: A Description of Egypt and Journal of the Famine Years, by ʿAbd al-Laṭīf al-Baghdādī
Edited and translated by Tim Mackintosh-Smith (2021)

The Book of Travels, by Ḥannā Diyāb
Edited by Johannes Stephan
Translated by Elias Muhanna (2 volumes; 2021)

Kalīlah and Dimnah: Fables of Virtue and Vice, by Ibn al-Muqaffaʿ
Edited by Michael Fishbein
Translated by Michael Fishbein and James E. Montgomery (2021)

Love, Death, Fame: Poetry and Lore from the Emirati Oral Tradition, by al-Māyidī ibn Ẓāhir
Edited and translated by Marcel Kurpershoek (2022)

The Essence of Reality: A Defense of Philosophical Sufism, by ʿAyn al-Quḍāt
Edited and translated by Mohammed Rustom (2022)

The Requirements of the Sufi Path: A Defense of the Mystical Tradition, by Ibn Khaldūn
Edited and translated by Carolyn Baugh (2022)

The Doctors' Dinner Party, by Ibn Buṭlān
Edited and translated by Philip F. Kennedy and Jeremy Farrell (2023)

Fate the Hunter: Early Arabic Hunting Poems
Edited and translated by James E. Montgomery (2023)

The Book of Monasteries, by al-Shābushtī
Edited and translated by Hilary Kilpatrick (2023)

In Deadly Embrace: Arabic Hunting Poems, by Ibn al-Muʿtazz
Edited and translated by James E. Montgomery (2023)

The Divine Names, by ʿAfīf al-Dīn al-Tilimsānī
Edited and translated by Yousef Casewit (2023)

Bedouin Poets of the Nafūd Desert, by Khalaf Abū Zwayyid, ʿAdwān al-Hirbīd, and ʿAjlān ibn Rmāl
Edited and translated by Marcel Kurpershoek (2024)

The Rules of Logic, by Najm al-Dīn al-Kātibī
Edited and translated by Tony Street (2024)

Najm al-dīn al-Kātibī's al-Risālah al-Shamsiyyah: An Edition and Translation with Commentary, by Tony Street (2024)

A Demon Spirit: Arabic Hunting Poems, by Abū Nuwās
Edited and translated by James E. Montgomery (2024)

Arabian Hero: Oral Poetry and Narrative Lore from Northern Arabia, by Shāyiʿ al-Amsaḥ
Edited and translated by Marcel Kurpershoek (2024)

The Genius of Invective: Ibn Zaydūn's Letter Explained, by Ibn Nubātah
Edited and translated by Peter Webb (2025)

English-only Paperbacks

Leg over Leg, by Aḥmad Fāris al-Shidyāq (2 volumes; 2015)

The Expeditions: An Early Biography of Muḥammad, by Maʿmar ibn Rāshid (2015)

The Epistle on Legal Theory: A Translation of al-Shāfiʿī's Risālah, by al-Shāfiʿī (2015)

The Epistle of Forgiveness, by Abū l-ʿAlāʾ al-Maʿarrī (2016)

The Principles of Sufism, by ʿĀʾishah al-Bāʿūniyyah (2016)

A Treasury of Virtues: Sayings, Sermons, and Teachings of ʿAlī, by al-Qāḍī al-Quḍāʿī with the *One Hundred Proverbs* attributed to al-Jāḥiẓ (2016)

The Life of Ibn Ḥanbal, by Ibn al-Jawzī (2016)

Mission to the Volga, by Ibn Faḍlān (2017)

Accounts of China and India, by Abū Zayd al-Sīrāfī (2017)

Consorts of the Caliphs: Women and the Court of Baghdad, by Ibn al-Sāʿī (2017)

A Hundred and One Nights (2017)

Disagreements of the Jurists: A Manual of Islamic Legal Theory, by al-Qāḍī al-Nuʿmān (2017)

What ʿĪsā ibn Hishām Told Us, by Muḥammad al-Muwayliḥī (2018)

War Songs, by ʿAntarah ibn Shaddād (2018)

The Life and Times of Abū Tammām, by Abū Bakr Muḥammad ibn Yaḥyā al-Ṣūlī (2018)

The Sword of Ambition, by ʿUthmān ibn Ibrāhīm al-Nābulusī (2019)

Brains Confounded by the Ode of Abū Shādūf Expounded: Volume One, by Yūsuf al-Shirbīnī (2019)

Brains Confounded by the Ode of Abū Shādūf Expounded: Volume Two, by Yūsuf al-Shirbīnī and *Risible Rhymes*, by Muḥammad ibn Maḥfūẓ al-Sanhūrī (2019)

The Excellence of the Arabs, by Ibn Qutaybah (2019)

Light in the Heavens: Sayings of the Prophet Muḥammad, by al-Qāḍī al-Quḍāʿī (2019)

Scents and Flavors: A Syrian Cookbook (2020)

Arabian Satire: Poetry from 18th-Century Najd, by Ḥmēdān al-Shwēʿir (2020)

In Darfur: An Account of the Sultanate and Its People, by Muḥammad al-Tūnisī (2020)

Arabian Romantic: Poems on Bedouin Life and Love, by Ibn Sbayyil (2020)

The Philosopher Responds: An Intellectual Correspondence from the Tenth Century, by Abū Ḥayyān al-Tawḥīdī and Abū ʿAlī Miskawayh (2021)

Impostures, by al-Ḥarīrī (2021)

The Discourses: Reflections on History, Sufism, Theology, and Literature—Volume One, by al-Ḥasan al-Yūsī (2021)

The Yoga Sutras of Patañjali, by Abū Rayḥān al-Bīrūnī (2022)

The Book of Charlatans, by Jamāl al-Dīn ʿAbd al-Raḥīm al-Jawbarī (2022)

The Book of Travels, by Ḥannā Diyāb (2022)

A Physician on the Nile: A Description of Egypt and Journal of the Famine Years, by ʿAbd al-Laṭīf al-Baghdādī (2022)

Kalīlah and Dimnah: Fables of Virtue and Vice, by Ibn al-Muqaffaʿ (2023)

Love, Death, Fame: Poetry and Lore from the Emirati Oral Tradition, by al-Māyidī ibn Ẓāhir (2023)

The Essence of Reality: A Defense of Philosophical Sufism, by ʿAyn al-Quḍāt (2023)

The Doctors' Dinner Party, by Ibn Buṭlān (2024)

The Requirements of the Sufi Path: A Defense of the Mystical Tradition, by Ibn Khaldūn (2024)

Fate the Hunter: Early Arabic Hunting Poems (2024)

The Book of Monasteries, by al-Shābushtī (2025)

In Deadly Embrace: Arabic Hunting Poems, by Ibn al-Muʿtazz (2025)

The Divine Names: A Mystical Theology of the Names of God in the Qurʾan, by ʿAfīf al-Dīn al-Tilimsānī (2025)

www.ingramcontent.com/pod-product-compliance
Ingram Content Group UK Ltd.
Pitfield, Milton Keynes, MK11 3LW, UK
UKHW041844170425
457600UK00002B/103

9 781479 835997